IEEE Standard Pascal
Computer Programming Language

Published by
The Institute of Electrical and Electronics Engineers, Inc

Distributed in cooperation with
Wiley-Interscience, a division of John Wiley & Sons, Inc

ANSI/IEEE
770 X3.97-1983

An American National Standard

IEEE Standard Pascal
Computer Programming Language

Joint Sponsors

IEEE Pascal Standards Committee
of the
IEEE Computer Society
and
ANSI/X3J9 of
American National Standards Committee X3

Approved September 17, 1981

IEEE Standards Board

Approved December 16, 1982

American National Standards Institute

Second Printing
April 1983

ISBN 0-471-88944-X

Library of Congress Catalog Number 82-84259

© Copyright 1979
Institute of Electrical and Electronics Engineers, Inc

© Copyright 1983
American National Standards Institute, Inc
and
Institute of Electrical and Electronics Engineers, Inc

Published by

**The Institute of Electrical and Electronics Engineers, Inc
345 East 47th Street, New York, NY 10017**

January 7, 1983   *SH08912*

Foreword

(This Foreword is not a part of ANSI/IEEE770X3.97-1983, IEEE Standard Pascal Computer Programming Language.)

This standard provides an unambiguous and machine independent definition of the language Pascal. Its purpose is to facilitate portability of Pascal programs for use on a wide variety of data processing systems.

Language History.

The computer programming language Pascal was designed by Professor Niklaus Wirth to satisfy two principal aims:

(1) To make available a language suitable for teaching programming as a systematic discipline based on certain fundamental concepts clearly and naturally reflected by the language.

(2) To define a language whose implementations could be reliable and efficient on then available computers.

However, it has become apparent that Pascal has attributes that go far beyond these original goals. It is now being increasingly used commercially in the writing of system and application software. This standard is primarily a consequence of the growing commercial interest in Pascal and the need to promote the portability of Pascal programs between data processing systems.

In drafting this standard the continued stability of Pascal has been a prime objective. However, apart from changes to clarify the specification, one major change has been introduced. The syntax used to specify procedural and functional parameters has been changed to require the use of a procedure or function heading, as appropriate (see 6.6.3.1); this change was introduced to overcome a language insecurity.

Project History.

(Throughout, the term JPC refers to the Joint ANSI/X3J9-IEEE Pascal Standards Committee.) In the fall of 1978 application was made to the IEEE Standards Board by the IEEE Computer Society to authorize project P770. After approval, the first meeting was held in January 1979.

In December of 1978, X3J9 convened as a result of a SPARC resolution to form a US TAG (Technical Advisory Group) for the ISO Pascal standardization effort initiated by the UK.

In agreement with IEEE representatives, in February of 1979, an X3 resolution combined the X3J9 and P770 committees into a single committee called the Joint ANSI/X3J9-IEEE Pascal Standards Committee. The first meeting as JPC was held in April 1979.

At its 7th meeting in April 1980, JPC reviewed the first draft of ISO dp7185 and submitted its technical comments as JPC/80-111 together with their recommendation to X3 that the US should vote "no, because" in light of these comments.

For a summary of other important events in the project's history, see the annual reports from 1979 through 1981. Two other significant events occurred in February 1981:

(1) JPC reviewed the second draft of ISO dp7185 and submitted its technical comments as JPC/81-42 together with their recommendation to X3 that the US should vote "yes, but" in light of those comments.

(2) JPC passed a motion to submit to TC letter ballot the ISO dp7185 second draft together with JPC/81-42 and JPC/81-41 which describes how the requirements for compliance with the dpANS and proposed IEEE Pascal standard differ from compliance with the ISO draft proposed standard.

Project Charter.

As X3J9, it approved SD-3 described its program of work to be:

(1) Maintain a liaison with the ISO, BSI, and IEEE committees to work toward a common working draft standard. This work should include review of those bodies' documents and forwarding of comments based on that review. The eventual draft proposed American National Standard Pascal shall be compatible with any ISO Pascal standard and identical in content with the jointly developed proposed IEEE Pascal standard.

(2) Provide a means for review of all Pascal standardization activities.

(3) Carry out the development of a Pascal standard.

(4) Identify and evaluate common existing practices in the area of Pascal extensions.

(5) Act as a liaison group with organizations interested in interpretation of American National Standard Pascal.

The resolution to form JPC clarified the dual function of the single joint committee to produce a dpANS and a proposed IEEE Pascal standard, identical in content.

Technical Development.

(1) *Technical Constraints by X3 or IEEE.* None.

(2) *Technical Alternatives Considered.* In view of the charter to maintain compatibility with "any ISO Pascal standard," technical alternatives, suggestions, and recommendations were submitted with US letter ballots on ISO draft proposals. These items were then resolved by Working Group 4 as part of the international standardization process.

(3) *Significant Technical Issues on which JPC was Initially Divided.* Divergent opinions on the technical issues concerning conformant arrays were forwarded as part of the US letter ballot comments (JPC/80-111, JPC/81-42). To resolve the issue within the JPC, the conformant arrays definition was removed from the proposed domestic standard. Therefore, extensions to the language that solve the conformant array issue are permitted in the same manner as any other extension.

(4) *Information Collection Techniques Employed to Obtain Broader Input Data.*

Working Draft 3 published April 1979 in IEEE Computer magazine

Working Draft 3 published January 1979 in Pascal News No 14

dp7185 First Draft published April 1980 in SIGPLAN Notices

dp7185 First Draft published May 1980 in Pascal News No 18

dp7185 Second Draft published December 1980 in Pascal News No 20

Comments received from public review were distributed to all JPC members and discussed as part of the technical review. These were also forwarded directly to the appropriate international body responsible for an ISO dp.

(5) *Related Domestic Effort.* X3J9 (an X3 Technical Committee) and IEEE P770 combined to form the Joint ANSI/X3J9-IEEE Pascal Standards Committee in early 1979. The joint collaboration contributed in the international development of ISO/7185, from which this standard was developed.

International.

The British Standards Institution (BSI) Committee OIS/5 has been our counterpart in the UK. They are the sponsoring body for the ISO dp for Pascal. There are similar active groups in Australia, Canada, France, Germany, Netherlands and Japan. The international liaisons on these committees have been kept informed of the US activity by being on the JPC mailing list. Also, these committees have assigned members to WG4, the international working group for Pascal.

Other Standards and their Relationship to an American National Standard and IEEE Pascal Standard.

ISO Pascal Standard. See the preceding section on **Project Charter** and the following section on **Differences.**

Differences of Technical Substance Between this Standard and the International Standard, as Represented by ISO/DIS 7185.

The differences of technical substance are:

(1) The domestic standard does not include the conformant array feature.

(2) The domestic standard specifies that extensions may alter the status of implementation-dependent features or errors. The ISO document prohibits extensions from altering the status of these items.

(3) The domestic standard specifies that the relationship, if any, between end-of-line and values of the char-type shall be implementation-dependent. The ISO document requires that end-of-line not be a value of the char-type.

(4) This standard specifies the ordering of evaluation, accessing, and binding of the parameters of **read, readln, write,** and **writeln.** The international standard does not address this areas, leaving it neither specified, implementation-defined, nor implementation-dependent.

At the time of adoption of this standard, the text of the international standard was observed to contain several errors of definition and several points of apparent technical ambiguity or lack of clarity. This standard embodies corrections to those errors, and embodies certain wording which clarifies the apparent ambiguities. These differences in manner of definition are not differences of technical substance.

The errors that are corrected in this standard are in the definition of:

(1) String-element alternatives

(2) Data-transfer procedure parameters types

(3) Lexicographic ordering

(4) Control-variable usage restrictions

The international standard appears to permit or require the repeated evaluation of the file that is referenced by I/O procedures and of the arrays that are referenced by the data-transfer procedures. A detailed analysis is required to determine that the international standard does not in fact permit such repeated evaluation. This standard states that requirement more explicitly.

Except as noted in the list above of *Differences of Technical Substance*, compliance with this standard is equivalent to compliance at level 0 with the international standard in the following sense:

(1) Any program complying with this standard complies at level 0 with the international standard

(2) Any program or processor complying at level 0 with the international standard complies with this standard

(3) Any processor complying at level 1 with the international standard complies with this standard if it is "able to process in a manner similar to that specified for errors any use of [the conformant-array feature]"

(4) Any processor complying with this standard and not providing an extension which covers part or all of the intent of the conformant-array feature complies at level 0 with the international standard

(5) Any processor complying with this standard and providing an extension covering part or all of the intent of the conformant-array feature complies at level 1 with the international standard if it also includes the conformant-array feature.

Additionally, a program which uses any extension does not comply with either standard.

Future Work.

An SD3 for extended Pascal has been approved by X3 to authorize future work.

Suggestions for the improvement of this standard are welcomed. These suggestions should be sent to

Secretary
IEEE Standards Board
345 East 47th Street
New York, NY 10017

When the IEEE Standards Board approved this standard on September 17, 1981, it had the following membership:

This standard was processed and approved for submittal to ANSI by the American National Standards Committee on Information Systems, X3. Committee approval of this standard does not necessarily imply that all committee members voted for its approval.

At the time it approved this standard, the X3 committee had the following members:

Organization	Name of Representative
Digital Equipment Corporation	Lois C. Frampton
	Gary. S. Robinson (*Alt*)
GUIDE International	Frank Kirshenbaum
	Leland Milligan (*Alt*)
General Services Administration	William C. Rinehuls
	Donald J. Page (*Alt*)
Harris Corporation	Sam Mathan
	David Abmayr (*Alt*)
Hewlett-Packard	Donald C. Loughry
Honeywell Information Systems	Thomas J. McNamara
	Alan Teubner (*Alt*)
IBM Corporation	Mary Anne Gray
	J. S. Wilson (*Alt*)
IEEE Communications Society	Thomas A. Varetoni
IEEE Computer Society	Robert Poston
	Robert S. Stewart (*Alt*)
Lawrence Berkeley Laboratory	James A. Baker
	Robert J. Harvey (*Alt*)
Life Office Management Association	John I. Burke
	James F. Foley, Jr. (*Alt*)
3M Company	R. C. Smith
Moore Business Forms	D. H. Oddy
NCR Corporation	Thomas W. Kern
	William E. Snyder (*Alt*)
National Bureau of Standards	Robert E. Rountree
	James H. Burrows (*Alt*)
National Communications System	Marshall L. Cain
	George W. White (*Alt*)
Perkin-Elmer Corporation	David Ellis
	David Saunders (*Alt*)
Prime Computer	Jeffrey C. Flowers
	Winfried A. Burke (*Alt*)
Professional Secretaries International	Jerome Heitman
	P. E. Pesce (*Alt*)
Recognition Technology Users Association	Herbert F. Schantz
	G. W. Wetzel (*Alt*)
SHARE, Inc.	Thomas B. Steel
	Daniel Schuster (*Alt*)
Society of Certified Data Processors	Thomas M. Kurihara
	Ardyn E. Dubnow (*Alt*)
Sperry Univac	Marvin W. Bass
	Charles D. Card (*Alt*)
Telephone Group	Henry L. Marchese
	J. A. Owen (*Alt*)
	Stewart M. Garland (*Alt*)
Texas Instruments, Inc.	Presley Smith
	Don Caraway (*Alt*)
Travelers Insurance Companies, Inc.	Joseph T. Brophy
US Department of Defense	William LaPlant
	Harry Pontius (*Alt*)
Wang Laboratories, Inc.	Carl W. Schwarcz
	Marsha Hayek (*Alt*)
Xerox Corporation	John L. Wheeler
	Arthur R. Machell (*Alt*)

The Joint ANSI/X3J9–IEEE Pascal Standards Committee, which developed this standard had the following members:

Carol Sledge, *Chairman*   Michael Hagerty*, *Vice Chairman*

David L. Reese, *Secretary*   Joe Cointment, *International Representative*

Michael Alexander	Steven Hobbs	David Peercy
Jeffrey Allen	Albert A. Hoffman	Robert C. B. Poon
Ed Barkmeyer	Robert Hutchins	David L. Presberg
W. Ashby Boaz	Rosa C. Hwang	William C. Price
Jack Boudreaux	Scott Jameson	Bruce Ravenel**
A. Winsor Brown	David Jones	David C. Robbins
Jerry R. Brookshire	Steen Jurs	Lynne Rosenthal
Tomas M. Burger	Mel Kanner	Tom Rudkin
David S. Cargo	John Kaufmann	Stephen C. Schwarm
Richard J. Cichelli	Leslie Klein	Rick Shaw
Roger Cox	Bruce Knobe	Barry Smith
Jean Danver	Dennis Kodimer	Rudeen S. Smith
Debra Deutsch	Ronald E. Kole	Bill Stackhouse
Bob Dietrich	Alan A. Kortesoja	Marius Troost***
Victor A. Folwarczny	Edward Krall	Thomas N. Turba
G. G. Gustafson	Robert Lange	Prescott K. Turner
Thomas Giventer	Rainer McCown	Howard Turtle
Hellmut Golde	Jim Miner	Robert Tuttle
David N. Gray	Eugene N. Miya	Richard C. Vile, Jr
Paul Gregory	Mark Molloy	Larry B. Weber
Charles E. Haynes	William Neuhauser	David Weil
Christopher Henrich	Dennis Nicholson	Thomas R. Wilcox
Steven Hiebert	Mark Overgaard	Thomas Wolfe
Ruth Higgins	Ted C. Park	Harvey Wohlwend
Charles Hill	Donald D. Peckham	Kenneth M. Zemrowski

    *   Chairman IEEE Pascal Committee
  ** Past Chairman IEEE Pascal Committee
*** Past Chairman X3J9 Committee

Others who contributed to the development of this standard are:
A. M. Addyman: Chairman BSI OIS/5 and Convener of ISO/TC 97/SC 5
/Working Group 4 Pascal
Members of ISO/TC 97/SC 5/Working Group 4 Pascal

Thomas N. Turba and Sperry Univac made major contributions to the publication of this edition by editing the approved draft and supplying typeset copy. Their assistance is acknowledged with gratitude.

This standard was derived from the 2nd revision of ISO dp7185 and has been updated to include changes to the 3rd revision of ISO dp7185 and responses to public comments on the first draft of ANSI/IEEE770X3.97–1983.

EDITORIAL NOTE: It is the normal convention to use italic type for algebraic quantities. Since the status of such quantities contained in this standard may or may not directly represent true variable quantities, this convention has not been adopted in this standard.

Contents

An American National Standard

IEEE Standard Pascal
Computer Programming Language

1. Scope

1.1. This standard specifies the semantics and syntax of the computer programming language Pascal by specifying requirements for a processor and for a conforming program.

1.2. This standard does not specify:

(a) the size or complexity of a program and its data that will exceed the capacity of any specific data processing system or the capacity of a particular processor, nor the actions to be taken when the corresponding limits are exceeded;

(b) the minimal requirements of a data processing system that is capable of supporting an implementation of a processor for Pascal;

(c) the method of activating the program-block or the set of commands used to control the environment in which a Pascal program is transformed and executed;

(d) the mechanism by which programs written in Pascal are transformed for use by a data processing system;

(e) the method for reporting errors or warnings;

(f) the typographical representation of a program published for human reading.

2. Reference

ISO 646 : The 7-bit coded character set for information processing interchange.

3. Definitions

For the purposes of this standard, the following definitions apply.

NOTE: To draw attention to language concepts, some terms are printed in italics on their first mention in this standard.

3.1. Error.   A violation by a program of the requirements of this standard that a processor is permitted to leave undetected.

NOTES:
(1) If it is possible to construct a program in which the violation or non–violation of this standard requires knowledge of the data read by the program or the implementation definition of implementation–defined features, then violation of that requirement is classified as an *error*. Processors may report on such violations of the requirement without such knowledge, but there always remain some cases that require execution or simulated execution, or proof procedures with the required knowledge. Requirements that can be verified without such knowledge are not classified as errors.
(2) Processors should attempt the detection of as many errors as possible, and to as complete a degree as possible. Permission to omit detection is provided for implementations in which the detection would be an excessive burden.

3.2. Extension.   A modification to Section 6 of the requirements of this standard that does not invalidate any program complying with this standard, as defined by Section 5.2, except by prohibiting the use of one or more particular spellings of identifiers.

3.3. Implementation–Defined.   Possibly   differing   between processors, but defined for any particular processor.

3.4. Implementation–Dependent.   Possibly   differing   between processors and not necessarily defined for any particular processor.

3.5. Processor.   A system or mechanism that accepts a program as input, prepares it for execution, and executes the process so defined with data to produce results.

NOTE: A processor may consist of an interpreter, a compiler and run–time system, or other mechanism, together with an associated host computing machine and operating system, or other mechanism for achieving the same effect. A compiler in itself, for example, does not constitute a processor.

4. Definitional Conventions

The metalanguage used in this standard to specify the syntax of the constructs is based on Backus–Naur Form. The notation has been modified from the original to permit greater convenience of description and to allow for iterative productions to replace recursive ones. Table 1 lists the meanings of the various metasymbols. Further specification of the constructs is given by prose and, in some cases, by equivalent program fragments. Any identifier that is defined in Section 6 as a required identifier shall denote the corresponding required entity by its occurrence in such a program fragment. In all other respects, any such program fragment is bound by any pertinent requirement of this standard.

Table 1.
Metalanguage Symbols

Metasymbol	Meaning
=	shall be defined to be
|	alternatively
.	end of definition
[x]	0 or 1 instance of x
| x |	0 or more instances of x
(x | y)	grouping: either of x or y
"xyz"	the terminal symbol xyz
meta–identifier	a non–terminal symbol

A meta–identifier shall be a sequence of letters and hyphens beginning with a letter.

A sequence of terminal and non–terminal symbols in a production implies the concatenation of the text that they ultimately represent. Within 6.1 this concatenation is direct; no characters shall intervene. In all other parts of this standard the concatenation is in accordance with the rules set out in 6.1.

The characters required to form Pascal programs shall be those implicitly required to form the tokens and separators defined in 6.1.

Use of the words *of, in, containing* and *closest–containing* when expressing a relationship between terminal or non–terminal symbols shall have the following meanings.

the x *of* a y: refers to the x occurring directly in a production defining y.

the x *in* a y: is synonymous with 'the x *of* a y'.

a y *containing* an x: refers to any y from which an x is directly or indirectly derived.

the y *closest–containing* an x: that y which contains an x but does not contain another y *containing* that x.

These syntactic conventions are used in Section 6 to specify certain syntactic requirements and also the contexts within which certain semantic specifications apply.

5. Compliance

5.1. Processors. A processor complying with the requirements of this standard shall:

(a) accept all the features of the language specified in Section 6 with the meanings defined in Section 6;

(b) *(This section intentionally left blank to preserve numbering with ISO dp7185.)*

(c) not require the inclusion of substitute or additional language elements in a program in order to accomplish a feature of the language that is specified in Section 6;

(d) be accompanied by a document that provides a definition of all implementation–defined features;

(e) be able to determine whether or not a program violates any requirement of this standard, where such a violation is not designated an error, and report the result of this determination to the user of the processor; in the case where the processor does not examine the whole program, the user shall be notified that the determination is incomplete whenever no violations have been detected in the program text examined;

(f) treat each violation that is designated an error in at least one of the following ways:

(1) there shall be a statement in an accompanying document that the error is not reported;

(2) the processor shall report during preparation of the program for execution that an occurrence of that error was possible;

(3) the processor shall report the error during preparation of the program for execution;

(4) the processor shall report the error during execution of the program, and terminate execution of the program;

and if any violations that are designated as errors are treated in the manner described in 5.1(f)(1), then a note referencing each such treatment shall appear in a separate section of the accompanying document;

(g) be accompanied by a document that separately describes any features accepted by the processor that are prohibited or not specified in Section 6: such extensions shall be described as being 'extensions to Pascal as specified by ANSI/IEEE770X3.97–1983';

(h) be able to process in a manner similar to that specified for errors any use of any such extension;

(i) be able to process in a manner similar to that specified for errors any use of an implementation–dependent feature.

NOTES:
(1) The phrase 'be able to' is used in 5.1 to permit the implementation of a switch with which the user may control the reporting.
(2) In cases where the compilation is aborted due to some limitation of tables, etc., an incomplete determination of the kind   No violations were detected, but the examination is incomplete.' will satisfy the requirements of Section 5.1(e). In a similar manner, an interpretive or direct execution processor may report an incomplete determination for a program of which all aspects have not been examined.

A processor that purports to comply, wholly or partially, with the requirements of this standard shall do so only in the following terms. A *compliance statement* shall be produced by the processor as a consequence of using the processor, or shall be included in accompanying documentation. If the processor complies in all respects with the requirements of this standard the compliance statement shall be:

> *<This processor> complies with the requirements of ANSI/IEEE770X3.97–1983.*

If the processor complies with some but not all of the requirements of this standard then it shall not use the above statement, but shall instead use the following compliance statement:

> *<This processor> complies with the requirements of ANSI/IEEE770X3.97–1983 with the following exceptions:*

> *<followed by a reference to, or a complete list of, the requirements of the standard with which the processor does not comply>.*

In both cases the text <This processor> shall be replaced by an unambiguous name identifying the processor.

NOTE: Processors that do not comply fully with the requirements of the standard are not required to give full details of their failures to comply in the compliance statement; a brief reference to accompanying documentation that contains a complete list in sufficient detail to identify the defects is sufficient.

5.2. Programs.   A program complying with the requirements of this standard shall:

(a) use only those features of the language specified in Section 6,

(b) not rely on any particular interpretation of implementation–dependent features.

NOTES:
 (1) A program that complies with the requirements of this standard may rely on particular implementation–defined values or features.
 (2) The requirements for compliant programs and compliant processors do not require that the results produced by a compliant program are always the same when processed by a compliant processor. They may be, or they may differ, depending on the program. A simple program to illustrate this is:

```
program x(output); begin writeln(maxint) end.
```

6. Requirements

6.1. Lexical Tokens.

NOTE: The syntax given in this subsection (6.1) describes the formation of lexical tokens from characters and the separation of these tokens, and therefore does not adhere to the same rules as the syntax in the rest of this standard.

6.1.1. General.
The lexical tokens used to construct Pascal programs shall be classified into special–symbols, identifiers, directives, unsigned–numbers, labels and character–strings. The representation of any letter (upper–case or lower–case, differences of font, etc.) occurring anywhere outside of a character–string (see 6.1.7) shall be insignificant in that occurrence to the meaning of the program.

    letter = "a" | "b" | "c" | "d" | "e" | "f" | "g" | "h" | "i" | "j" | "k" | "l" | "m" |
              "n" | "o" | "p" | "q" | "r" | "s" | "t" | "u" | "v" | "w" | "x" | "y" | "z" .

    digit =   "0" | "1" | "2" | "3" | "4" | "5" | "6" | "7" | "8" | "9" .

6.1.2. Special–Symbols.
The special–symbols are tokens having special meanings and shall be used to delimit the syntactic units of the language.

    special-symbol = "+" | "-" | "*" | "/" | "=" | "<" | ">" | "[" |
                     "]" | "." | "," | ":" | ";" | "↑" | "(" | ")" | "<>" |
                     "<=" | ">=" | ":=" | ".." | word-symbol .

    word-symbol = "and" | "array" | "begin" | "case" | "const" | "div" |
                  "do" | "downto" | "else" | "end" | "file" | "for" |
                  "function" | "goto" | "if" | "in" | "label" | "mod" |
                  "nil" | "not" | "of" | "or" | "packed" | "procedure" |
                  "program" | "record" | "repeat" | "set" | "then" |
                  "to" | "type" | "until" | "var" | "while" | "with" .

6.1.3. Identifiers.
Identifiers may be of any length. All characters of an identifier shall be significant in distinguishing between identifiers. No identifier shall have the same spelling as any word–symbol. Identifiers that are specified to be *required* shall have special significance (see 6.2.2.10 and 6.10).

    identifier = letter { letter | digit } .

EXAMPLES:

> X   time   readinteger   WG4 AlterHeatSetting
> InquireWorkstationTransformation
> InquireWorkstationIdentification

6.1.4. Directives.   A   directive   shall   occur   only   *in*   a
procedure–declaration or function–declaration. The directive forward
shall be the only required directive (see 6.6.1 and 6.6.2). No directive shall
have the same spelling as any word–symbol.

> directive = letter { letter | digit } .

NOTE: Many processors provide, as an extension, the directive external, which is used to specify
that the procedure-block or function-block corresponding to that procedure-heading or
function-heading is external to the program-block. Usually it is in a library in a form to be input
to, or that has been produced by, the processor.

6.1.5. Numbers.   An unsigned–integer shall denote in decimal
notation a value of integer–type (see 6.4.2.2).   An unsigned–real shall
denote in decimal notation a value of real–type (see 6.4.2.2). The letter 'e'
preceding a scale factor shall mean *times ten to the power of.* The value
denoted by an unsigned–integer shall be in the closed interval 0 to maxint
(see 6.4.2.2 and 6.7.2.2).

> signed–number = signed–integer | signed–real .

> signed–real = [sign] unsigned–real .

> signed–integer = [sign] unsigned–integer .

> unsigned–number = unsigned–integer | unsigned–real .

> sign = "+" | "–" .

> unsigned–real =
>   unsigned–integer "." fractional–part ["e" scale–factor] |
>   unsigned–integer "e" scale–factor .

> unsigned–integer = digit–sequence .

> fractional–part = digit–sequence .

scale–factor = signed–integer .

digit–sequence = digit { digit } .

EXAMPLES:

   1e10   1   +100   −0.1   5e–3   87.35E+8

6.1.6. Labels. Labels shall be digit–sequences and shall be distinguished by their apparent integral values and shall be in the closed interval 0 to 9999.

label = digit–sequence .

6.1.7. Character–Strings. A character–string *containing* a single string–element shall denote a value of the required char–type (see 6.4.2.2). A character–string *containing* more than one string–element shall denote a value of a string–type (see 6.4.3.2) with the same number of components as the character–string *contains* string–elements. There shall be an implementation–defined one–to–one correspondence between the set of alternatives from which string–elements are drawn and a subset of the values of the required char–type. The occurrence of a string–element in a character–string shall denote the occurrence of the corresponding value of char–type.

character–string = "'" string–element { string–element } "'" .

string–element = apostrophe–image | string–character .

apostrophe–image = "''" .

string–character = one–of–a–set–of–implementation–defined–characters .

NOTE: Conventionally, the apostrophe–image is regarded as a substitute for the apostrophe character, which cannot be a string–character.

EXAMPLES:

  'A'   ';'   ''''
  'Pascal'   'THIS IS A STRING'

6.1.8. Token Separators.   The construct

˝{˝ any–sequence–of–characters–and–separation–of–lines–not–containing–right–brace ˝}˝

shall be a comment if the / does not occur within a character–string or within a comment. The substitution of a space for a comment shall not alter the meaning of a program.

Comments, spaces (except in character–strings), and the separation of consecutive lines shall be considered to be token separators. Zero or more token separators may occur between any two consecutive tokens, or before the first token of a program text. There shall be at least one separator between any pair of consecutive tokens made up of identifiers, word–symbols, labels or unsigned–numbers. No separators shall occur within tokens.

6.1.9. Lexical Alternatives.   The representation for lexical tokens and separators given in 6.1.1 to 6.1.8 shall constitute a *reference representation* for these tokens and separators. The reference representation shall be used for program interchange.

To facilitate the use of Pascal on processors that do not support the reference representation, the following alternatives have been defined. All processors that have the required characters in their character set shall provide both the reference representations and the alternative representations, and the corresponding tokens or separators shall not be distinguished.

The alternative representations for the tokens shall be:

Reference token	Alternative token
↑	@
[	(.
]	.)

NOTE: The character ^ that appears in some national variants of ISO 646 is regarded as identical to the character ↑. In this standard, the character ↑ has been used because of its greater visibility.

The alternative forms of comment shall be all forms of comment where one or both of the following substitutions are made:

Delimiting character	Alternative delimiting pair of characters
{	(*
}	*)

NOTES:
(1) A comment may thus commence with { and end with *), or commence with (* and end with } .
(2) If the sequence (*) occurs in a comment, it is equivalent to {} and marks the end of the comment, because the substitution is only for a delimiting character.
(3) See also 1.2(f).

6.2. Blocks, Scope and Activations.

6.2.1. Block.

A block *closest-containing* a label-declaration-part *in* which a label occurs shall *closest-contain* exactly one statement *in* which that label occurs. The occurrence of a label *in* the label-declaration-part *of* a block shall be its defining-point as a label for the region that is the block.

```
block = label-declaration-part
            constant-definition-part
             type-definition-part
               variable-declaration-part
                 procedure-and-function-declaration-part
                   statement-part .
```

label-declaration-part = ["label" label { "," label } ";"] .

constant-definition-part =
    ["const" constant-definition ";" { constant-definition ";" }] .

type-definition-part =
    ["type" type-definition ";" { type-definition ";" }] .

variable-declaration-part =
    ["var" variable-declaration ";" { variable-declaration ";" }] .

procedure-and-function-declaration-part =
    { (procedure-declaration | function-declaration) ";" } .

The statement-part shall specify the algorithmic actions to be executed upon an activation of the block.

statement-part = compound-statement .

6.2.2. Scope.

6.2.2.1. Each identifier or label *contained* by the program-block shall have a defining-point.

6.2.2.2. Each defining-point shall have a region that is a part of the program text, and a scope that is a part or all of that region.

6.2.2.3. The region of each defining-point is defined elsewhere (see 6.2.1, 6.2.2.10, 6.3, 6.4.1, 6.4.2.3, 6.4.3.3, 6.5.1, 6.5.3.3, 6.6.1, 6.6.2, 6.6.3.1, 6.8.3.10, 6.10).

6.2.2.4. The scope of each defining-point shall be its region (including all regions enclosed by that region) subject to 6.2.2.5 and 6.2.2.6.

6.2.2.5. When an identifier or label has a defining-point for region A and another identifier or label having the same spelling has a defining-point for some region B enclosed by A, then region B and all regions enclosed by B shall be excluded from the scope of the defining-point for region A.

6.2.2.6. The region that is the field-specifier *of* a field-designator shall be excluded from the enclosing scopes.

6.2.2.7. When an identifier or label has a defining-point for a region, another identifier or label with the same spelling shall not have a defining-point for that region.

6.2.2.8. Within the scope of a defining-point of an identifier or label, each occurrence of an identifier or label having the same spelling as the identifier or label of the defining-point shall be designated an *applied occurrence* of the identifier or label of the defining-point, except for an occurrence that constituted the defining-point of that identifier or label; such an occurrence shall be designated a *defining occurrence*. No occurrence outside that scope shall be an applied occurrence.

NOTE: Within the scope of a defining-point of an identifier or label, there are no applied occurrences of an identifier or label that cannot be distinguished from it and have a defining-point for a region enclosing that scope.

6.2.2.9. The defining–point of an identifier or label shall precede all applied occurrences of that identifier or label *contained* by the program–block with one exception, namely that an identifier may have an applied occurrence in the type–identifier *of* the domain–type *of* any new–pointer–types *contained* by the type–definition–part that *contains* the defining–point of the type–identifier.

6.2.2.10. Identifiers that denote required constants, types, procedures and functions shall be used as if their defining–points have a region enclosing the program (see 6.1.3, 6.3, 6.4.1 and 6.6.4.1).

NOTE: The required identifiers input and output are not included, since these denote variables.

6.2.2.11. Whatever an identifier or label denotes at its defining–point shall be denoted at all applied occurrences of that identifier or label.

NOTE: Within syntax definitions, an applied occurrence of an identifier is qualified, e.g. type–identifier, whereas a use that constitutes a defining–point is not qualified.

6.2.3. Activations.

6.2.3.1. A procedure–identifier or function–identifier having a defining–point for a region that is a block within the procedure–and–function–declaration–part of that block shall be designated *local* to that block.

6.2.3.2. The activation of a block shall contain:

(a) for the statement–part *of* the block, an algorithm, the completion of which shall terminate the activation (see also 6.8.2.4);

(b) for each label *in* a statement having a defining–point in the label–declaration–part of the block, a program–point in the algorithm of the activation at that statement;

(c) for each variable–identifier having a defining–point for the region that is the block, a variable possessing the type associated with the variable–identifier;

(d) for each procedure–identifier local to the block, a procedure with the procedure–block corresponding to the procedure–identifier, and the formal parameters of that procedure–block;

(e) for each function-identifier local to the block, a function with the function-block corresponding to, and the result type associated with, the function-identifier, and the formal parameters of that function-block;

(f) if the block is a function-block, a result possessing the associated result type.

NOTE: Each activation contains its own algorithm, set of program-points, set of variables, set of procedures, and set of functions, distinct from every other activation.

6.2.3.3. The activation of a procedure or function shall be the activation of the block of its procedure-block or function-block, respectively, and shall be designated as *within*:

(a) the activation containing the procedure or function; and

(b) all activations that that containing activation is within.

NOTE: An activation of a block B can only be within activations of blocks containing B. Thus an activation is not within another activation of the same block.

Within an activation, an applied occurrence of a label or variable-identifier, or of a procedure-identifier or function-identifier local to the block of the activation, shall denote the corresponding program-point, variable, procedure, or function, respectively, of that activation; except that the function-identifier *of* an assignment-statement shall, within an activation of the function denoted by that function-identifier, denote the result of that activation.

6.2.3.4. A procedure-statement or function-designator contained in the algorithm of an activation and that specifies the activation of a block shall be designated the activation-point of that activation of the block.

6.2.3.5. All variables contained by an activation, except for those listed as program-parameters, and any result of an activation, shall be totally-undefined at the commencement of that activation. The algorithm, program-points, variables, procedures and functions, if any, shall exist until the termination of the activation.

6.3. Constant–Definitions. A constant–definition shall introduce an identifier to denote a value.

    constant-definition = identifier "=" constant .

    constant = [sign] (unsigned-number | constant-identifier) |
            character-string .

    constant-identifier = identifier .

The occurrence of an identifier *in* a constant–definition *of* a constant–definition–part *of* a block shall constitute its defining–point for the region that is the block. The constant *in* a constant–definition shall not contain an applied occurrence of the identifier *in* the constant–definition. Each applied occurrence of that identifier shall be a constant–identifier and shall denote the value denoted by the constant *of* the constant–definition. A constant–identifier *in* a constant containing an occurrence of a sign shall have been defined to denote a value of real–type or of integer–type. The required constant–identifiers shall be as specified in 6.4.2.2 and 6.7.2.2.

6.4. Type–Definitions.

6.4.1. General. A type–definition shall introduce an identifier to denote a type. Type shall be an attribute that is possessed by every value and every variable. Each occurrence of a new–type shall denote a type that is distinct from any other new–type.

    type-definition = identifier "=" type-denoter .

    type-denoter = type-identifier | new-type .

    new-type = new-ordinal-type |
            new-structured-type |
            new-pointer-type .

The occurrence of an identifier *in* a type–definition *of* a type–definition–part *of* a block shall constitute its defining–point for the region that is the block. Each applied occurrence of that identifier shall be a type–identifier and shall denote the same type as that which is denoted by the type-denoter *of* the type-definition. Except for applied occurrences in the domain-type *of* a new-pointer-type, the type-denoter shall not contain an applied occurrence of the identifier *in* the type-definition.

Types shall be classified as simple, structured or pointer types. The required type-identifiers and corresponding required types shall be as specified in 6.4.2.2 and 6.4.3.5.

    simple-type-identifier = type-identifier .

    structured-type-identifier = type-identifier .

    pointer-type-identifier = type-identifier .

    type-identifier = identifier .

A type-identifier shall be considered as a simple-type-identifier, a structured-type-identifier, or a pointer-type-identifier, according to the type that it denotes.

6.4.2. Simple-Types.

6.4.2.1. General.   A simple-type shall determine an ordered set of values. The values of each ordinal-type shall have integer ordinal numbers. An ordinal-type-identifier shall denote an ordinal-type.

    simple-type = ordinal-type | real-type-identifier .

    ordinal-type = new-ordinal-type | ordinal-type-identifier .

    new-ordinal-type = enumerated-type | subrange-type .

    ordinal-type-identifier = type-identifier .

    real-type-identifier = type-identifier .

6.4.2.2. Required Simple-Types.   The following types shall exist:

(a) *integer-type* .   The required ordinal-type-identifier integer shall denote the integer-type.   The values shall be a subset of the whole numbers, denoted as specified in 6.1.5 by signed-integer (see also 6.7.2.2). The ordinal number of a value of integer-type shall be the value itself.

(b) _real-type_. The required real–type–identifier real shall denote the real–type. The values shall be an implementation–defined subset of the real numbers denoted as specified in 6.1.5 by signed–real.

(c) _Boolean-type_. The required ordinal–type–identifier Boolean shall denote the Boolean–type. The values shall be the enumeration of truth values denoted by the required constant–identifiers false and true, such that false is the predecessor of true. The ordinal numbers of the truth values denoted by false and true shall be the integer values 0 and 1 respectively.

(d) _char-type_. The required ordinal–type–identifier char shall denote the char–type. The values shall be the enumeration of a set of implementation–defined characters, some possibly without graphic representations. The ordinal numbers of the character values shall be values of integer–type, that are implementation–defined, and that are determined by mapping the character values on to consecutive non–negative integer values starting at zero. The mapping shall be order preserving. The following relations shall hold.

(1) The subset of character values representing the digits 0 to 9 shall be numerically ordered and contiguous.

(2) The subset of character values representing the upper–case letters A to Z, if available, shall be alphabetically ordered but not necessarily contiguous.

(3) The subset of character values representing the lower–case letters a to z, if available, shall be alphabetically ordered but not necessarily contiguous.

(4) The ordering relationship between any two character values shall be the same as between their ordinal numbers.

NOTE: Operators applicable to the required simple–types are specified in 6.7.2.

6.4.2.3. Enumerated–Types.

An enumerated–type shall determine an ordered set of values by enumeration of the identifiers that denote those values. The ordering of these values shall be determined by the sequence in which their identifiers are enumerated, i.e. if x precedes y then x is less than y. The ordinal number of a value that is of an enumerated–type shall be determined by mapping all the values of the type on to consecutive

non–negative values of integer–type starting from zero. The mapping shall
be order preserving.

enumerated–type = "(" identifier–list ")" .

identifier–list = identifier { "," identifier } .

The occurrence of an identifier *in* the identifier–list *of* an
enumerated–type shall constitute its defining–point as a
constant–identifier for the region that is the block *closest–containing* the
enumerated–type.

EXAMPLES:

(red, yellow, green, blue, tartan)
(club, diamond, heart, spade)
(married, divorced, widowed, single)
(scanning, found, notpresent)
(Busy, InterruptEnable, ParityError, OutOfPaper, LineBreak)

6.4.2.4. Subrange–Types. A subrange–type shall include
identification of the smallest and the largest value in the subrange. The
first constant *of* a subrange–type shall specify the smallest value, and this
shall be less than or equal to the largest value which shall be specified by
the other constant *of* the subrange–type. Both constants shall be of the
same ordinal–type, and that ordinal–type shall be designated the host type
of the subrange–type.

subrange–type = constant ".." constant .

EXAMPLES:

1..100
–10..+10
red..green
'0'..'9'

6.4.3. Structured–Types.

6.4.3.1. General. A new–structured–type shall be classified as an
array–type, record–type, set–type or file–type according to the
unpacked–structured–type *closest–contained* by the new–structured–type.
A component of a value of a structured–type shall be a value.

structured–type = new–structured–type | structured–type–identifier .

new–structured–type = ["packed"] unpacked–structured–type .

unpacked–structured–type = array–type | record–type |
set–type | file–type .

The occurrence of the token packed *in* a new–structured–type shall designate the type denoted thereby as *packed*. The designation of a structured–type as packed shall indicate to the processor that data–storage of values should be economized, even if this causes operations on, or accesses to components of, variables possessing the type to be less efficient in terms of space or time.

The designation of a structured–type as packed shall affect the representation in data–storage of that structured–type only; i.e., if a component is itself structured, the component's representation in data–storage shall be packed only if the type of the component is designated packed.

NOTE: The ways in which the treatment of entities of a type is affected by whether or not the type is designated packed are specified in 6.4.3.2, 6.4.5, 6.6.3.3, 6.6.5.4 and 6.7.1.

6.4.3.2. Array–Types.

An array–type shall be structured as a mapping from each value specified by its index–type on to a distinct component. Each component shall have the type denoted by the type–denoter *of* the component–type *of* the array–type.

array–type =
"array" "[" index–type | "," index–type | "]" "of" component–type .

index–type = ordinal–type .

component–type = type–denoter .

EXAMPLES:

array [1..100] of real
array [Boolean] of colour

37

An array-type that specifies a sequence of two or more index-types shall be an abbreviated notation for an array-type specified to have as its index-type the first index-type in the sequence, and to have a component-type that is an array-type specifying the sequence of index-types without the first and specifying the same component-type as the original specification. The component-type thus constructed shall be designated packed if and only if the original array-type is designated packed. The abbreviated form and the full form shall be equivalent.

NOTE: Each of the following two examples thus contains different ways of expressing its array-type.

EXAMPLE 1.

    array [Boolean] of array [1..10] of array [size] of real
    array [Boolean] of array [1..10, size] of real
    array [Boolean, 1..10, size] of real
    array [Boolean, 1..10] of array [size] of real

EXAMPLE 2.

    packed array [1..10, 1..8] of Boolean
    packed array [1..10] of packed array [1..8] of Boolean

Let i denote a value of the index-type; let v[i] denote a value of that component of the array-type that corresponds to the value i by the structure of the array-type; let the smallest and largest values specified by the index-type be denoted by m and n; and let $k = (ord(n)-ord(m)+1)$ denote the number of values specified by the index-type; then the values of the array-type shall be the distinct k-tuples of the form

    $(v[m], ... , v[n])$.

NOTE: A value of an array-type does not therefore exist unless all of its component values are defined. If the component-type has c values, then it follows that the cardinality of the set of values of the array-type is c raised to the power k.

Any type designated packed and denoted by an array-type having as its index-type a denotation of a subrange-type specifying a smallest value of 1 and a largest value of greater than 1, and having as its component-type a denotation of the char-type, shall be designated a *string-type*.

The correspondence of character–strings to values of string–types is obtained by relating the individual string–elements of the character–string, taken in textual order, to the components of the values of the string–type in order of increasing index.

NOTE: The values of a string–type possess additional properties which allow writing them to textfiles (see 6.9.3.6) and define their use with relational–operators (see 6.7.2.5).

6.4.3.3. Record–Types.   The structure and values of a record–type shall be the structure and values of the field–list *of* the record–type.

  record–type = "record" field–list "end" .

  field–list = [(fixed–part [";" variant–part] | variant–part) [";"]] .

  fixed–part = record–section { ";" record–section } .

  record–section = identifier–list ":" type–denoter .

  variant–part = "case" variant–selector "of" variant { ";" variant } .

  variant–selector = [tag–field ":"] tag–type .

  tag–field = identifier .

  variant = case–constant–list ":" "(" field–list ")" .

  tag–type = ordinal–type–identifier .

  case–constant–list = case–constant { "," case–constant } .

  case–constant = constant .

A field–list that *contains* neither a fixed–part nor a variant–part shall have no components, shall define a single null value, and shall be designated *empty*.

The occurrence of an identifier *in* the identifier–list *of* a record–section *of* a fixed–part *of* a field–list shall constitute its defining–point as a field–identifier for the region that is the record–type *closest–containing* the field–list, and shall associate the field–identifier with a distinct component, which shall be designated a *field.* of the record–type and of the field–list. That component shall have the type denoted by the type–denoter *of* the record–section.

The field–list *closest–containing* a variant–part shall have a distinct component that shall have the values and structure defined by the variant–part.

Let V_i denote the value of the i–th component of a non–empty field–list having m components; then the values of the field–list shall be distinct m–tuples of the form

$$(V_1, V_2, ..., V_m).$$

NOTE: If the type of the i–th component has F_i values, then the cardinality of the set of values of the field–list shall be $(F_1 * F_2 * ... * F_m)$.

A tag–type shall denote the type denoted by the ordinal–type–identifier *of* the tag–type. A case–constant shall denote the value denoted by the constant *of* the case–constant.

The type of each case–constant *in* the case–constant–list *of* a variant *of* a variant–part shall be compatible with the tag–type *of* the variant–selector *of* the variant–part. The values denoted by all case–constants of a type that is required to be compatible with a given tag–type shall be distinct and the set thereof shall be equal to the set of values specified by the tag–type. The values denoted by the case–constants *of* the case–constant–list *of* a variant shall be designated as corresponding to the variant.

With each variant–part shall be associated a type designated the selector–type possessed by the variant–part. If the variant–selector *of* the variant–part *contains* a tag–field, or if the case–constant–list *of* each variant *of* the variant–part *contains* only one case–constant, then the selector–type shall be denoted by the tag–type, and each variant *of* the variant–part shall be associated with those values specified by the selector–type denoted by the case–constants *of* the case–constant–list *of* the variant. Otherwise, the selector–type possessed by the variant–part shall be a new ordinal–type constructed such that there is exactly one value of the type for each variant *of* the variant–part, and no others, and each variant shall be associated with a distinct value of that type.

Each variant–part shall have a component that shall be designated the *selector* of the variant–part, and which shall possess the selector–type of the variant–part. If the variant–selector *of* the variant–part *contains* a tag–field, then the occurrence of an identifier *in* the tag–field shall constitute the defining–point of the identifier as a field–identifier for the region that is the record–type *closest-containing* the variant–part, and shall associate the field–identifier with the selector of the variant–part. The selector shall be designated a field of the record–type if and only if it is associated with a field–identifier.

Each variant *of* a variant–part shall denote a distinct component of the variant–part; the component shall have the values and structure of the field–list *of* the variant, and shall be associated with those values specified by the selector–type possessed by the variant–part associated with the variant. The value of the selector of the variant–part shall cause the associated variant and component of the variant–part to be in a state that shall be designated *active*.

The values of a variant–part shall be the distinct pairs

$$(k, X_k)$$

where k represents a value of the selector of the variant–part, and X_k is a value of the field–list *of* the active variant *of* the variant–part.

NOTES:

(1) If there are n values specified by the selector–type, and if the field–list of the variant associated with the i–th value has T_i values, then the cardinality of the set of values of the variant–part is $(T_1 + T_2 + ... + T_n)$. There is no component of a value of a variant–part corresponding to any non–active variant of the variant–part.

(2) Restrictions placed on the use of fields of a record–variable pertaining to variant–parts are specified in 6.5.3.3, 6.6.3.3 and 6.6.5.3.

EXAMPLES:

(1)   record
            year : 0..2000;
            month : 1..12;
            day : 1..31
        end

(2)   record
          name, firstname : string;
          age : 0..99;
          case married : Boolean of
          true : (Spousesname : string);
          false : ()
       end

(3)   record
          x, y : real;
          area : real;
          case shape of
          triangle :
             (side : real;
             inclination, angle1, angle2 : angle);
          rectangle :
             (side1, side2 : real;
             skew : angle);
          circle :
             (diameter : real);
       end

6.4.3.4. Set-Types.   A set-type shall determine the set of values that
is structured as the powerset of the base-type *of* the set-type. Thus each
value of a set-type shall be a set whose members shall be unique values
of the base-type.

   set-type = "set" "of" base-type .

   base-type = ordinal-type .

NOTE: Operators applicable to values of set-types are specified in 6.7.2.4.

EXAMPLES:

   set of char
   set of (club, diamond, heart, spade)

NOTE: If the base-type of a set-type has b values then the cardinality of the set of values is 2
raised to the power b.

For every ordinal–type S, there exists an unpacked set type designated the *unpacked canonical set–of–T type* and there exists a packed set type designated the *packed canonical set–of–T type.* If S is a subrange–type then T is the host type of S; otherwise T is S. Each value of the type set of S is also a value of the unpacked canonical set–of–T type, and each value of the type packed set of S is also a value of the packed canonical set–of–T type.

6.4.3.5. File–Types.

NOTE: A file–type describes sequences of values of the specified component–type, together with a current position in each sequence and a mode that indicates whether the sequence is being inspected or generated.

file–type = "file" "of" component–type .

A type–denoter shall not be permissible as the component–type *of* a file–type if it denotes either a file–type or a structured–type having any component whose type–denoter is not permissible as the component–type *of* a file–type.

EXAMPLES:

file of real
file of vector

A file–type shall define implicitly a type designated a *sequence–type* having exactly those values, which shall be designated *sequences.* defined by the following five rules in items (a) to (e).

NOTE: The notation x∼y represents the concatenation of sequences x and y. The explicit representation of sequences (e.g. S(c)), of concatenation of sequences, of the first, last and rest selectors, and of sequence equality is not part of the Pascal language. These notations are used to define file values, below, and the required file operations in 6.6.5.2 and 6.6.6.5.

(a) S() shall be a value of the sequence–type S, and shall be designated the *empty sequence.* The empty sequence shall have no components.

(b) Let c be a value of the specified component–type, and let x be a value of the sequence–type S; then S(c) shall be a sequence of type S, consisting of the single component value c, and both S(c)∼x and x∼S(c) shall be sequences, distinct from S(), of type S.

(c) Let c, S, and x be as in (b); let y denote the sequence $S(c) \sim x$; and let z denote the sequence $x \sim S(c)$; then the notation y.first shall denote c (i.e., the first component value of y), y.rest shall denote x (i.e., the sequence obtained from y by deleting the first component), and z.last shall denote c (i.e., the last component value of z).

(d) Let x and y each be a non-empty sequence of type S; then $x = y$ shall be true if and only if both (x.first = y.first) and (x.rest = y.rest) are true. If x or y is the empty sequence, then $x = y$ shall be true if and only if both x and y are the empty sequence.

(e) Let x, y, and z be sequences of type S; then $x \sim (y \sim z) = (x \sim y) \sim z$, $S() \sim x = x$, and $x \sim S() = x$ shall be true.

A file-type also shall define implicitly a type designated a *mode-type* having exactly two values which are designated *Inspection* and *Generation*.

NOTE: The explicit denotation of the values Inspection and Generation is not part of the Pascal language.

A file-type shall be structured as three components. Two of these components, designated f.L and f.R, shall be of the implicit sequence-type. The third component, designated f.M, shall be of the implicit mode-type.

Let f.L and f.R each be a single value of the sequence-type; let f.M be a single value of the mode-type; then each value of the file-type shall be a distinct triple of the form

    (f.L, f.R, f.M)

where f.R shall be the empty sequence if f.M is the value Generation. The value, f, of the file-type shall be designated empty if and only if $f.L \sim f.R$ is the empty sequence.

NOTE: The two components, f.L and f.R, of a value of the file-type may be considered to represent the single sequence $f.L \sim f.R$ together with a current position in that sequence. If f.R is non-empty, then f.R.first may be considered the current component as determined by the current position; otherwise, the current position is designated the end-of-file position.

There shall be a file-type that is denoted by the required structured-type-identifier text. The structure of the type denoted by text shall define an additional sequence-type whose values shall be designated *lines.* A line shall be a sequence cs~S(e), where cs is a sequence of components having the char-type, and e represents a special component value, which shall be designated an *end-of-line,* and which shall be indistinguishable from the char value space except by the required function eoln (see 6.6.6.5) and by the required procedures reset (see 6.6.5.2), writeln (see 6.9.4), and page (sec 6.9.5). If l is a line then no component of l other than l.last shall be an end-of-line. These provisions describe the functionality only, and shall not be construed to determine in any way the underlying representation of textfiles; in particular, the relationship, if any, between end-of-line and values of the char-type shall be implementation-dependent.

A line-sequence, ls, shall be either the empty sequence or the sequence l~ls' where l is a line and ls' is a line-sequence.

Every value t of the type denoted by text shall satisfy one of the following two rules.

(a) If t.M = Inspection, then t.L~t.R shall be a line-sequence.

(b) If t.M = Generation, then t.L~t.R shall be ls~cs, where ls is a line-sequence and cs is a sequence of components possessing the char-type.

NOTE: In rule (b), cs may be considered, especially if it is non-empty, to be a partial line that is being generated. Such a partial line cannot occur during inspection of a file. Also, cs does not correspond to t.R since t.R is the empty sequence if t.M = Generation.

A variable that possesses the type denoted by the required structured-type-identifier text shall be designated a *textfile.*

NOTE: All required procedures and functions applicable to a variable of type *file of char* are applicable to textfiles. Additional required procedures and functions, applicable only to textfiles, are defined in 6.6.6.5 and 6.9.

6.4.4. Pointer–Types. The values of a pointer–type shall consist of a single nil–value, and a set of identifying–values each identifying a distinct variable possessing the domain–type *of* the pointer–type. The set of identifying–values shall be dynamic, in that the variables and the values identifying them may be created and destroyed during the execution of the program. Identifying–values and the variables identified by them shall be created only by the required procedure new (see 6.6.5.3).

NOTE: Since the nil–value is not an identifying–value it does not identify a variable.

The token nil shall denote the nil–value in all pointer–types.

pointer-type = new-pointer-type | pointer-type-identifier .

new-pointer-type = "↑" domain-type .

domain-type = type-identifier .

NOTE: The token nil does not have a single type, but assumes a suitable pointer–type to satisfy the assignment–compatibility rules, or the compatibility rules for operators, if possible.

6.4.5. Compatible Types. Types T1 and T2 shall be designated *compatible* if any of the following four statements is true.

(a) T1 and T2 are the same type.

(b) T1 is a subrange of T2, or T2 is a subrange of T1, or both T1 and T2 are subranges of the same host type.

(c) T1 and T2 are set–types of compatible base–types, and either both T1 and T2 are designated packed or neither T1 nor T2 is designated packed.

(d) T1 and T2 are string–types with the same number of components.

6.4.6. Assignment–Compatibility. A value of type T2 shall be designated *assignment-compatible* with a type T1 if any of the following five statements is true.

(a) T1 and T2 are the same type and that type is permissible as the component–type *of* a file–type (see 6.4.3.5).

(b) T1 is the real–type and T2 is the integer–type.

(c) T1 and T2 are compatible ordinal–types and the value of type T2 is in the closed interval specified by the type T1.

(d) T1 and T2 are compatible set–types and all the members of the value of type T2 are in the closed interval specified by the base–type of T1.

(e) T1 and T2 are compatible string–types.

At any place where the rule of assignment–compatibility is used:

(1) it shall be an error if T1 and T2 are compatible ordinal–types and the value of type T2 is not in the closed interval specified by the type T1;

(2) it shall be an error if T1 and T2 are compatible set–types and any member of the value of type T2 is not in the closed interval specified by the base–type of the type T1.

6.4.7. Example of a type–definition–part.

```
type
    natural = 0..maxint;
    count = integer;
    range = integer;
    colour = (red, yellow, green, blue);
    sex = (male, female);
    year = 1900..1999;
    shape = (triangle, rectangle, circle);
    punchedcard = array [1..80] of char;
    charsequence = file of char;
    polar = record
                    r : real;
                    theta : angle
                end;
    indextype = 1..limit;
    vector = array [indextype] of real;
    person = ↑persondetails;
```

```
      persondetails =
        record
          name, firstname : charsequence;
          age : integer;
          married : Boolean;
          father, child, sibling : person;
          case s : sex of
            male :
              (enlisted, bearded : Boolean);
            female :
              (mother, programmer : Boolean)
        end;
      FileOfInteger = file of integer;
```

NOTE: In the above example *count, range* and *integer* denote the same type. The types denoted
by *year* and *natural* are compatible with, but not the same as, the type denoted by *range, count*
and *integer*.

6.5. Declarations and Denotations of Variables.

6.5.1. Variable–Declarations.   A variable shall be an entity to
which a value may be attributed (see 6.8.2.2). Each identifier *in* the
identifier–list *of* a variable–declaration shall denote a distinct variable
possessing the type denoted by the type–denoter *of* the
variable–declaration.

        variable-declaration = identifier-list ":" type-denoter .

The occurrence of an identifier *in* the identifier-list *of* a
variable-declaration *of* the variable-declaration-part *of* a block shall
constitute its defining-point as a variable-identifier for the region that is
the block. The structure of a variable possessing a structured-type shall
be the structure of the structured-type. A use of a variable-access shall
be an access, at the time of the use, to the variable thereby denoted. A
variable-access, according to whether it is an entire-variable, a
component-variable, an identified-variable, or a buffer-variable, shall
denote a declared variable, a component of a variable, a variable which is
identified by a pointer value (see 6.4.4), or a buffer-variable, respectively.

        variable-access = entire-variable | component-variable |
                    identified-variable | buffer-variable .

Example of a variable–declaration–part:

```
var
    x, y, z, max : real;
    i, j : integer;
    k : 0..9;
    p, q, r : Boolean;
    operator : (plus, minus, times);
    a : array [0..63] of real;
    c : colour;
    f : file of char;
    hue1, hue2 : set of colour;
    p1, p2 : person;
    m, m1, m2 : array [1..10, 1..10] of real;
    coord : polar;
    pooltape : array [1..4] of FileOfInteger;
    date : record
                month : 1..12;
                year : integer
            end;
```

NOTE: Variables occurring in examples in the remainder of this standard should be assumed to have been declared as specified in 6.5.1.

6.5.2. Entire–Variables.

entire–variable = variable–identifier .

variable–identifier = identifier .

6.5.3. Component–Variables.

6.5.3.1. General.   A component of a variable shall be a variable. A component–variable shall denote a component of a variable. A reference, or access to a component of a variable shall constitute a reference, or access, respectively, to the variable. The value, if any, of the component of a variable shall be the same component of the value, if any, of the variable.

component–variable = indexed–variable | field–designator .

6.5.3.2. Indexed–Variables.   A component of a variable possessing
an array–type shall be denoted by an indexed–variable.

   indexed–variable =
       array–variable "[" index–expression { "," index–expression } "]" .

   array–variable = variable–access .

   index–expression = expression .

An array–variable shall be a variable–access that denotes a variable
possessing an array–type. For an indexed–variable *closest–containing* a
single index–expression, the value of the index–expression shall be
assignment–compatible with the index–type *of* the array–type. The
component denoted by the indexed–variable shall be the component that
corresponds to the value of the index–expression by the mapping of the
type possessed by the array–variable (see 6.4.3.2).

EXAMPLES:

   a[12]
   a[i + j]
   m[k]

If the array–variable is itself an indexed–variable an abbreviation may
be used. In the abbreviated form, a single comma shall replace the
sequence]*[* that occurs in the full form. The abbreviated form and the
full form shall be equivalent.

The order of evaluation of the index–expressions *of* an indexed–variable
shall be implementation–dependent.

EXAMPLES:

   m[k][1]
   m[k, 1]

NOTE: These two examples denote the same component variable.

6.5.3.3. **Field–Designators.** A field–designator either shall denote that component of the record–variable *of* the field–designator associated with the field–identifier *of* the field–specifier *of* the field–designator, by the record–type possessed by the record–variable; or shall denote the variable denoted by the field–designator–identifier (see 6.8.3.10) *of* the field–designator. A record–variable shall be a variable–access that denotes a variable possessing a record–type.

The occurrence of a record–variable *in* a field–designator shall constitute the defining–point of the field–identifiers associated with components of the record–type possessed by the record–variable, for the region that is the field–specifier *of* the field–designator.

```
field-designator = record-variable "." field-specifier |
                   field-designator-identifier .

record-variable = variable-access .

field-specifier = field-identifier .

field-identifier = identifier .
```

EXAMPLES:

```
p2↑.mother
coord.theta
```

An access to a component of a variant *of* a variant–part, where the selector of the variant–part is not a field, shall attribute to the selector that value specified by its type associated with the variant.

It shall be an error unless a variant is active for the entirety of each reference and access to each component of the variant.

When a variant becomes not active, all of its components shall become totally–undefined.

NOTE: If the selector of a variant–part is undefined, then no variant of the variant–part is active.

6.5.4. Identified-Variables.

An identified-variable shall denote the variable (if any) identified by the value of the pointer-variable *of* the identified-variable (see 6.4.4 and 6.6.5.3).

identified-variable = pointer-variable "↑" .

pointer-variable = variable-access .

A variable created by the required procedure new (see 6.6.5.3) shall be accessible until the termination of the activation of the program-block or until the variable is made inaccessible (see the required procedure dispose, 6.6.5.3).

NOTE: The accessibility of the variable also depends on the existence of a pointer-variable that has attributed to it the corresponding identifying value.

A pointer-variable shall be a variable-access that denotes a variable possessing a pointer-type. It shall be an error if the pointer-variable *of* an identified-variable either denotes a nil-value or is undefined. It shall be an error to remove from its pointer-type the identifying-value of an identified-variable (see 6.6.5.3) when a reference to the identified variable exists.

EXAMPLES:

p1↑
p1↑.father↑
p1↑.sibling↑.father↑

6.5.5. Buffer-Variables.

A file-variable shall be a variable-access that denotes a variable possessing a file-type. A buffer-variable shall denote a variable associated with the variable denoted by the file-variable *of* the buffer-variable. A buffer-variable associated with a textfile shall possess the char-type; otherwise, a buffer-variable shall possess the component-type *of* the file-type possessed by the file-variable *of* the buffer-variable.

buffer-variable = file-variable "↑" .

file-variable = variable-access .

EXAMPLES:

input↑
pooltape[2]↑

It shall be an error to alter the value of a file–variable f when a reference to the buffer–variable f↑ exists. A reference or access to a buffer–variable shall constitute a reference or access, respectively, to the associated file–variable.

6.6. Procedure and Function Declarations.

6.6.1. Procedure–Declarations.

procedure–declaration = procedure–heading ";" directive |
                       procedure–identification ";" procedure–block |
                       procedure–heading ";" procedure–block .

procedure–heading = "procedure" identifier [formal–parameter–list] .

procedure–identification = "procedure" procedure–identifier .

procedure–identifier = identifier .

procedure–block = block .

The occurrence of a formal–parameter–list *in* a procedure–heading *of* a procedure–declaration shall define the formal parameters of the procedure–block, if any, associated with the identifier *of* the procedure–heading to be those of the formal–parameter–list.

The occurrence of an identifier *in* the procedure–heading *of* a procedure–declaration shall constitute its defining–point as a procedure–identifier for the region that is the block *closest–containing* the procedure–declaration.

Each identifier having a defining–point as a procedure–identifier in a procedure–heading *of* a procedure–declaration *closest–containing* the directive forward shall have exactly one of its applied occurrences in a procedure–identification *of* a procedure–declaration, and that shall be *closest–contained* by the procedure–and–function–declaration–part *closest–containing* the procedure–heading.

The occurrence of a procedure–block *in* a procedure–declaration shall associate the procedure–block with the identifier *in* the procedure–heading, or with the procedure–identifier *in* the procedure–identification, *of* the procedure–declaration.

Example of a procedure–and–function–declaration–part:

```
procedure readinteger (var f : text; var x : integer);
var
  i : natural;
begin
  while f↑ = ' ' do get(f);
  {The file buffer contains the first non–space char}
  i := 0;
  while f↑ in ['0'..'9'] do
  begin
    i := (10 * i) + (ord(f↑) – ord('0'));
    get(f)
  end;
  {The file buffer contains a non–digit}
  x := i
  {Of course if there are no digits, x is zero}
end;


procedure bisect (function f(x : real) : real;
  a, b : real;
  var result : real);
{This procedure attempts to find a zero of f(x) in (a,b) by
  the method of bisection.  It is assumed that the procedure is
  called with suitable values of a and b such that
      (f(a) < 0) and (f(b) > 0)
  The estimate is returned in the last parameter.}
const
  Eps = 1e–10;
var
  midpoint : real;
```

```
begin
  {The invariant P is true by calling assumption}
  midpoint := a;
  while abs(a - b) > Eps * abs(a) do
    begin
    midpoint := (a + b) / 2;
    if f(midpoint) < 0 then a := midpoint
    else b := midpoint
    {Which re-establishes the invariant:
      P = (f(a) < 0) and (f(b) > 0)
      and reduces the interval (a,b) provided that the
      value of midpoint is distinct from both a and b.}
  end;
  {P together with the loop exit condition assures that a zero
    is contained in a small sub-interval.  Return the midpoint as
    the zero.}
  result := midpoint
end;

procedure PrepareForAppending (var f : FileOfInteger);
{This procedure takes a file in an arbitrary state and sets
  it up in a condition for appending data to its end.  Simpler
  conditioning is only possible if assumptions are made about the
  initial state of the file.}
var
  LocalCopy : FileOfInteger;

    procedure CopyFiles (var from, into : FileOfInteger);
    begin
      reset(from); rewrite(into);
      while not eof(from) do
      begin
        into↑ := from↑;
        put(into); get(from)
      end
    end { of CopyFiles };

begin { of body of PrepareForAppending }
  CopyFiles(f, LocalCopy);
  CopyFiles(LocalCopy, f)
end { of PrepareForAppending };
```

6.6.2. Function-Declarations.

function-declaration = function-heading ";" directive |
                       function-identification ";" function-block |
                       function-heading ";" function-block .

function-heading =
     "function" identifier [formal-parameter-list] ":" result-type .

function-identification = "function" function-identifier .

function-identifier = identifier .

result-type = simple-type-identifier | pointer-type-identifier .

function-block = block .

The occurrence of a formal-parameter-list *in* a function-heading *of* a function-declaration shall define the formal parameters of the function-block, if any, associated with the identifier *of* the function-heading to be those of the formal-parameter-list. The function-block shall *contain* at least one assignment-statement such that the function-identifier *of* the assignment-statement is associated with the block (see 6.8.2.2).

The occurrence of an identifier *in* the function-heading *of* a function-declaration shall constitute its defining-point as a function-identifier associated with the result type denoted by the result-type for the region that is the block *closest-containing* the function-declaration.

Each identifier having a defining-point as a function-identifier in the function-heading *of* a function-declaration *closest-containing* the directive forward shall have exactly one of its applied occurrences in a function-identification *of* a function-declaration, and that shall be *closest-contained* by the procedure-and-function-declaration-part *closest-containing* the function-heading.

The occurrence of a function-block *in* a function-declaration shall associate the function-block with the identifier *in* the function-heading, or with the function-identifier *in* the function-identification, *of* the function–declaration; the block of the function–block shall be associated with the result type that is associated with the identifier or function–identifier, respectively.

Example of a procedure–and–function–declaration–part:

```
function Sqrt (x : real) : real;

{This function computes the square root of x (x > 0) using Newton's
method.}
var
   old, estimate : real;
begin
   estimate := x;
   repeat
      old := estimate;
      estimate := (old + x / old) * 0.5;
   until abs(estimate - old) < Eps * estimate;
   {Eps being a global constant}
   Sqrt := estimate
end { of Sqrt };

function max (a : vector) : real;
{This function finds the largest component of the value of a.}
var
   largestsofar : real;
   fence : indextype;
begin
   largestsofar := a[1];
   {Establishes largestsofar = max(a[1])}
   for fence := 2 to limit do begin
      if largestsofar < a[fence] then largestsofar := a[fence]
      {Re-establishing largestsofar = max(a[1], ... ,a[fence])}
   end;
   {So now largestsofar = max(a[1], ... ,a[limit])}
   max := largestsofar
end { of max };

function GCD (m, n : natural) : natural;
begin
   if n=0 then GCD := m else GCD := GCD(n, m mod n);
end;
```

{The following two functions analyze a parenthesized expression and convert it to an internal form. They are declared forward since they are mutually recursive, i.e. they call each other.}

```
function ReadExpression : formula;
   forward;

function ReadOperand : formula;
   forward;

function ReadExpression; {See forward declaration of heading.}
   var
      this : formula;
      op : operation;
   begin
   this := ReadOperand;
   while IsOperator(nextsym) do
      begin
      op := ReadOperator;
      this := MakeFormula(this, op, ReadOperand);
      end;
   ReadExpression := this
   end;

function ReadOperand; {See forward declaration of heading.}
   begin
      if IsOpenParenthesis(nextsym) then
      begin
      SkipSymbol;
      ReadOperand := ReadExpression;
      {nextsym should be a close-parenthesis}
      SkipSymbol
      end
   else ReadOperand := ReadElement
   end;
```

6.6.3. Parameters.

6.6.3.1. General. The identifier–list *in* a value–parameter–specification shall be a list of value parameters. The identifier–list *in* a variable–parameter–specification shall be a list of variable parameters.

```
formal-parameter-list =
    "(" formal-parameter-section { ";" formal-parameter-section } ")" .

formal-parameter-section = value-parameter-specification |
                           variable-parameter-specification |
                           procedural-parameter-specification |
                           functional-parameter-specification .

value-parameter-specification = identifier-list ":" type-identifier .

variable-parameter-specification =
          "var" identifier-list ":" type-identifier .

procedural-parameter-specification = procedure-heading .

functional-parameter-specification = function-heading .
```

An identifier defined to be a parameter–identifier for the region that is the formal–parameter–list *of* a procedure–heading shall be designated a formal parameter of the block *of* the procedure–block, if any, associated with the identifier *of* the procedure–heading. An identifier defined to be a parameter–identifier for the region that is the formal–parameter–list *of* a function–heading shall be designated a formal parameter of the block *of* the function–block, if any, associated with the identifier *of* the function–heading.

The occurrence of an identifier *in* the identifier–list *of* a value–parameter–specification or a variable–parameter–specification shall constitute its defining–point as a parameter–identifier for the region that is the formal–parameter–list *closest–containing* it and its defining–point as the associated variable–identifier for the region that is the block, if any, of which it is a formal parameter.

The occurrence of the identifier *of* a procedure–heading *in* a procedural–parameter–specification shall constitute its defining–point as a parameter-identifier for the region that is the formal-parameter-list *closest-containing* it and its defining-point as the associated procedure-identifier for the region that is the block, if any, of which it is a formal parameter.

The occurrence of the identifier *of* a function-heading *in* a functional-parameter-specification shall constitute its defining-point as a parameter-identifier for the region that is the formal-parameter-list *closest-containing* it and its defining-point as the associated function-identifier for the region that is the block, if any, of which it is a formal parameter.

NOTE: If the formal-parameter-list is *contained* in a procedural-parameter-specification or a functional-parameter-specification, there is no corresponding procedure-block or function-block.

6.6.3.2. Value Parameters.

The formal parameter and its associated variable-identifier shall denote the same variable. The formal parameter shall possess the type denoted by the type-identifier *of* the value-parameter-specification. The type possessed by a formal parameter shall be one that is permitted as the component-type *of* a file-type. The actual-parameter (see 6.7.3 and 6.8.2.3) shall be an expression whose value is assignment-compatible with the type possessed by the formal parameter. The current value of the expression shall be attributed upon activation of the block to the variable that is denoted by the formal parameter.

6.6.3.3. Variable Parameters.

The actual-parameter shall be a variable-access. The type possessed by the actual-parameters shall be the same as that denoted by the type-identifier *of* the variable-parameter-specification, and the formal parameters shall also possess that type. The actual-parameter shall be accessed before the activation of the block, and this access shall establish a reference to the variable thereby accessed during the entire activation of the block; the corresponding formal parameter and its associated variable-identifier shall denote the referenced variable during the activation.

An actual variable parameter shall not denote a field that is the selector of a variant-part. An actual variable parameter shall not denote a component of a variable where that variable possesses a type that is designated packed.

6.6.3.4. Procedural Parameters.

The actual-parameter (see 6.7.3 and 6.8.2.3) shall be a procedure-identifier that has a defining-point *contained* by the program-block. The procedure denoted by the actual-parameter and the procedure denoted by the formal parameter shall have congruous formal-parameter-lists (see 6.6.3.6) if either has a formal-parameter-list. The formal parameter and its associated procedure-identifier shall denote the actual parameter during the entire activation of the block.

6.6.3.5. Functional Parameters.

The actual-parameter (see 6.7.3 and 6.8.2.3) shall be a function-identifier that has a defining-point *contained* by the program-block. The function denoted by the actual-parameter and the function denoted by the formal parameter shall have the same result-type and shall have congruous formal-parameter-lists (see 6.6.3.6) if either has a formal-parameter-list. The formal parameter and its associated function-identifier shall denote the actual parameter during the entire activation of the block.

NOTE: Since required procedures and functions are used as if their defining-points have a region enclosing the program (see 6.2.2.10), these procedures and functions may not be used as actual parameters in a program.

6.6.3.6. Parameter List Congruity.

Two formal-parameter-lists shall be congruous if they contain the same number of formal-parameter-sections and if the formal-parameter-sections in corresponding positions match. Two formal-parameter-sections shall match if any of the following statements is true.

(a) They are both value-parameter-specifications containing the same number of parameters and the type-identifier *in* each value-parameter-specification denotes the same type.

(b) They are both variable-parameter-specifications containing the same number of parameters and the type-identifier *in* each variable-parameter-specification denotes the same type.

(c) They are both procedural-parameter-specifications and the formal-parameter-lists *of* the procedure-headings thereof are congruous.

(d) They are both functional-parameter-specifications, the formal-parameter-lists *of* the function-headings thereof are congruous, and the type-identifiers *of* the result-types of the function-headings thereof denote the same type.

6.6.4. Required Procedures and Functions.

6.6.4.1. General.
The required procedure–identifiers and function–identifiers and the corresponding required procedures and functions shall be as specified in 6.6.5 and 6.6.6, respectively.

NOTE: Required procedures and functions do not necessarily follow the rules given elsewhere for procedures and functions.

6.6.5. Required Procedures.

6.6.5.1. General.
The required procedures shall be file handling procedures, dynamic allocation procedures and transfer procedures.

6.6.5.2. File Handling Procedures.
Except for the application of rewrite or reset to the program parameters denoted by input or output, the effects of applying each of the file handling procedures rewrite, put, reset and get to a file–variable f shall be defined by pre–assertions and post–assertions about f, its components f.L, f.R, and f.M, and about the associated buffer–variable f↑. The use of the variable f0 within an assertion shall be considered to represent the state or value, as appropriate, of f prior to the operation, while f (within an assertion) shall denote the variable after the operation, and similarly for f0↑ and f↑.

It shall be an error if the stated pre–assertion does not hold immediately prior to any use of the defined operation. It shall be an error if any variable explicitly denoted in an assertion of equality is undefined. The post–assertion shall hold prior to the next subsequent access to the file, its components, or its associated buffer–variable. The post–assertions imply corresponding activities on the external entities, if any, to which the file–variables are bound. These activities, and the point at which they are actually performed, shall be implementation–defined.

rewrite(f)   pre–assertion: true.

           post–assertion: $(f.L = f.R = S())$ and
$(f.M = Generation)$ and
$(f↑$ is totally–undefined).

put(f)   pre–assertion: $(f0.M = Generation)$ and
$(f0.L$ is not undefined) and
$(f0.R = S())$ and
$(f0↑$ is not undefined).

	post–assertion:	(f.M = Generation) and (f.L = (f0.L~S(f0↑))) and (f.R = S()) and (f↑ is totally–undefined).
reset(f)	pre–assertion:	The components f0.L and f0.R are not undefined.
	post–assertion:	(f.L = S()) and (f.R = (f0.L~f0.R~X)) and (f.M = Inspection) and (if f.R = S() then (f↑ is totally–undefined) else (f↑ = f.R.first)),

where, if f possesses the type denoted by the required structured–type–identifier text and if f0.L~f0.R is not empty and if (f0.L~f0.R).last is not designated an end–of–line, then X shall be a sequence having an end–of–line component as its only component; otherwise X = S().

get(f)	pre–assertion:	(f0.M = Inspection) and (neither f0.L nor f0.R are undefined) and (f0.R <> S()).
	post–assertion:	(f.M = Inspection) and (f.L = (f0.L~S(f0.R.first))) and (f.R = f0.R.rest) and (if f.R = S() then (f↑ is totally–undefined) else (f↑ = f.R.first)).

When the file–variable f possesses a type other than that denoted by text, the required procedures read and write shall be defined as follows.

read   Let f denote a file–variable and $v_1 \ldots v_n$ denote variable–accesses; then the procedure–statement read(f,v_1, ... , v_n) shall access the file variable and establish a reference to the file variable for the remaining execution of the statement. The execution of the statement shall be equivalent to

begin read(ff,v_1); read(ff,v_2,...,v_n) end

63

where ff denotes the referenced file variable. The read statement containing v_1 shall be executed before accessing the variables $v_2,...,v_n$.

Let f be a file–variable and v be a variable–access; then the procedure–statement read(f,v) shall access the file variable and establish a reference to that file variable for the remaining execution of the statement. The execution of the statement shall be equivalent to

begin v := ff↑; get(ff) end

where ff denotes the referenced file variable.

NOTE: The variable–access is not a variable parameter. Consequently it may be a component of a packed structure and the value of the buffer–variable need only be assignment–compatible with it.

write   Let f denote a file–variable and $e_1 ... e_n$ denote expressions; then the procedure–statement write(f,e_1, ... , e_n) shall access the file variable and establish a reference to that file variable for the remaining execution of the statement. The execution of the statement shall be equivalent to

begin write(ff,e_1); write(ff,e_2,...,e_n) end

where ff denotes the referenced file variable. The write statement containing e_1 shall be executed before evaluating the expressions $e_2,...,e_n$.

Let f be a file–variable and e be an expression; then the procedure–statement write(f,e) shall access the file variable and establish a reference to that file variable for the remaining execution of the statement. The execution of the write statement shall be equivalent to

begin ff↑ := e; put(ff) end

where ff denotes the referenced file variable.

NOTES:
(1) The required procedures **read, write, readln, writeln** and **page**, as applied to textfiles, are described in 6.9.
(2) Since the definitions of **read** and **write** include the use of **get** and **put**, the implementation–defined aspects of their post–assertions also apply.

6.6.5.3. Dynamic Allocation Procedures.

new(p)

shall create a new variable that is totally–undefined, shall create a new identifying–value of the pointer–type associated with p, that identifies the new variable, and shall attribute this identifying–value to the variable denoted by the variable–access p. The created variable shall possess the type that is the domain–type *of* the pointer–type possessed by p.

$new(p,c_1,...,c_n)$

shall create a new variable that is totally–undefined, shall create a new identifying–value of the pointer–type associated with p, that identifies the new variable, and shall attribute this identifying–value to the variable denoted by the variable–access p. The created variable shall possess the record–type that is the domain–type *of* the pointer–type possessed by p and shall have

nested variants that correspond to the case–constants $c_1,...,c_n$. The case–constants shall be listed in order of increasing nesting of the variant–parts. Any variant not specified shall be at a deeper level of nesting than that specified by c_n. It shall be an error if a variant *of* a variant–part within the new variable becomes active and a different variant *of* the variant–part is one of the specified variants.

dispose(q)

shall remove the identifying–value denoted by the expression q from the pointer–type of q. It shall be an error if the identifying–value had been created using the form $new(p,c_1,...,c_n)$.

$dispose(q,k_1,...,k_m)$

shall remove the identifying–value denoted by the expression q from the pointer–type of q. The case–constants $k_1,...,k_m$ shall be listed in order of increasing nesting of the variant–parts. It shall be an error if the variable had been created using the form $new(p,c_1,...,c_n)$ and m is not equal to n. It shall be an error if the variants in the variable identified by the pointer–value of q are different from those specified by the case–constants $k_1,...,k_m$.

NOTE: The removal of an identifying–value from the pointer–type to which it belongs renders the identified variable inaccessible (see 6.5.4) and makes undefined all variables and functions that have that value attributed (see 6.6.3.2 and 6.8.2.2).

It shall be an error if q has a nil–value or is undefined.

It shall be an error if a variable created using the second form of **new** is accessed by the identified–variable *of* the variable–access *of* a factor, *of* an assignment–statement, or *of* an actual–parameter.

6.6.5.4. Transfer Procedures.   Let a be a variable possessing an array–type, and let s1 denote the index–type thereof, let z be a variable possessing an array–type designated packed, let s2 denote the index–type thereof, and let the array–types have the same component–type; let u and v be the smallest and largest values of the type s2, let i be an expression whose value is assignment–compatible with s1, and let j and k denote auxiliary variables which the program does not otherwise contain. The type possessed by j shall be s2; the type possessed by k shall be s1.

The statement pack(a,i,z) shall access the array variables a and z and establish references to these variables for the remaining execution of the statement. The execution of the statement shall be equivalent to

```
begin
k := i;
for j := u to v do
  begin
  zz[j] := aa[k];
  if j <> v then k := succ(k)
  end
end
```

where aa denotes the referenced unpacked array variable and zz denotes the referenced packed array variable.

The statement unpack(z,a,i) shall access the array variables a and z and establish references to these variables for the remaining execution of the statement. The execution of the statement shall be equivalent to

```
begin
k := i;
for j := u to v do
  begin
  aa[k] := zz[j];
  if j < > v then k := succ(k)
  end
end
```

where aa denotes the referenced unpacked array variable and zz denotes the referenced packed array variable.

6.6.6. Required Functions.

6.6.6.1. General.
The required functions shall be arithmetic functions, transfer functions, ordinal functions and Boolean functions.

6.6.6.2. Arithmetic Functions.
For the following arithmetic functions, the expression x shall be either of real-type or integer-type. For the functions abs and sqr, the type of the result shall be the same as the type of the parameter, x. For the remaining arithmetic functions, the result shall always be of real-type.

Function	Result
abs(x)	shall compute the absolute value of x.
sqr(x)	shall compute the square of x. It shall be an error if such a value does not exist.
sin(x)	shall compute the sine of x, where x is in radians.
cos(x)	shall compute the cosine of x, where x is in radians.
exp(x)	shall compute the value of the base of natural logarithms raised to the power x.
ln(x)	shall compute the natural logarithm of x, if x is greater than zero. It shall be an error if x is not greater than zero.
sqrt(x)	shall compute the non-negative square root of x, if x is not negative. It shall be an error if x is negative.
arctan(x)	shall compute the principal value, in radians, of the arctangent of x.

6.6.6.3. Transfer Functions.

trunc(x) From the expression x that shall be of real–type, this function
shall return a result of integer–type. The value of trunc(x)
shall be such that if x is positive or zero then
$0<=x-trunc(x)<1$; otherwise $-1<x-trunc(x)<=0$. It shall be
an error if such a value does not exist.

EXAMPLES:
  trunc(3.5) yields 3
  trunc(–3.5) yields –3

round(x) From the expression x that shall be of real–type, this function
shall return a result of integer–type. If x is positive or zero,
round(x) shall be equivalent to trunc(x+0.5), otherwise
round(x) shall be equivalent to trunc(x–0.5). It shall be an
error if such a value does not exist.

EXAMPLES:
  round(3.5) yields 4
  round(–3.5) yields –4

6.6.6.4. Ordinal Functions.

ord(x) From the expression x that shall be of an ordinal–type, this
function shall return a result of integer–type that shall be the
ordinal number (see 6.4.2.2 and 6.4.2.3) of the value of the
expression x.

chr(x) From the expression x that shall be of integer–type, this
function shall return a result of char–type that shall be the
value whose ordinal number is equal to the value of the
expression x if such a character value exists. It shall be an
error if such a character value does not exist.

For any value, ch, of char–type, it shall be true that:
  chr(ord(ch)) = ch

succ(x) From the expression x that shall be of an ordinal–type, this
function shall return a result that shall be of the same type
as that of the expression (see 6.7.1). The function shall yield
a value whose ordinal number is one greater than that of the

expression x, if such a value exists. It shall be an error if such a value does not exist.

pred(x)   From the expression x that shall be of an ordinal–type, this function shall return a result that shall be of the same type as that of the expression (see 6.7.1). The function shall yield a value whose ordinal number is one less than that of the expression x, if such a value exists. It shall be an error if such a value does not exist.

6.6.6.5. Boolean Functions.

odd(x)   From the expression x that shall be of integer–type, this function shall be equivalent to the expression (abs(x) mod 2 = 1).

eof(f)   The parameter f shall be a file–variable; if the actual–parameter–list is omitted, the function shall be applied to the required textfile input (see 6.10). When eof(f) is activated, it shall be an error if f is undefined; otherwise the function shall yield the value true if f.R is the empty sequence (see 6.4.3.5), otherwise false.

eoln(f)   The parameter f shall be a textfile; if the actual–parameter–list is omitted, the function shall be applied to the required textfile input (see 6.10). When eoln(f) is activated, it shall be an error if f is undefined or if eof(f) is true; otherwise the function shall yield the value true if f.R.first is an end–of–line component (see 6.4.3.5), otherwise false.

6.7. Expressions.

6.7.1. General.   An expression shall denote a value unless a variable denoted by a variable-access *contained* by the expression is undefined at the time of its use, in which case that use shall be an error. The use of a variable-access as a factor shall denote the value, if any, attributed to the variable accessed thereby. Operator precedences shall be according to four classes of operators as follows. The operator not shall have the highest precedence, followed by the multiplying-operators, then the adding-operators and signs, and finally, with the lowest precedence, the relational-operators. Sequences of two or more operators of the same precedence shall be left associative.

expression =
    simple-expression [relational-operator simple-expression] .

simple-expression = [sign] term { adding-operator term } .

term = factor { multiplying-operator factor } .

factor = variable-access | unsigned-constant | function-designator |
    set-constructor | "(" expression ")" | "not" factor .

unsigned-constant = unsigned-number | character-string |
    constant-identifier | "nil" .

set-constructor =
    "[" [member-designator { "," member-designator }] "]" .

member-designator = expression [".." expression] .

Any factor whose type is S, where S is a subrange of T, shall be treated as of type T. Similarly, any factor whose type is set of S shall be treated as of the unpacked canonical set-of-T type, and any factor whose type is packed set of S shall be treated as of the packed canonical set-of-T type.

NOTE: Consequently, an expression that consists of a single factor of type S is itself of type T, and an expression that consists of a single factor of type set of S is itself of type set of T, and an expression that consists of a single factor of type packed set of S is itself of type packed set of T.

A set-constructor shall denote a value of a set-type. The set-constructor [ ] shall denote that value in every set-type that contains no members. A set-constructor *containing* one or more member-designators shall denote either a value of the unpacked canonical set-of-T type or, if the context so requires, the packed canonical set-of-T type, where T is the type of every expression *of* each member-designator *of* the set-constructor. The type T shall be an ordinal-type. The value denoted by the set-constructor shall contain zero or more members each of which shall be denoted by at least one member-designator *of* the set-constructor.

The member-designator x, where x is an expression, shall denote the member that shall have the value x. The member-designator x..y, where x and y are expressions, shall denote zero or more members that shall have the values of the base-type in the closed interval from the value of x to the value of y. The order of evaluation of the expressions *of* a member–designator shall be implementation–dependent. The order of evaluation of the member–designators *of* a set–constructor shall be implementation–dependent.

NOTE: The member–designator x..y denotes no members if the value of x is greater than the value of y.

EXAMPLES:

(a) Factors:
x
15
(x + y + z)
sin(x + y)
[red, c, green]
[1, 5, 10..19, 23]
not p

(b) Terms:
x * y
i / (1 – i)
(x <= y) and (y < z)

(c) Simple expressions:
p or q
x + y
–x
hue1 + hue2
i * j + 1

(d) Expressions:
x = 1.5
p <= q
p = q and r
(i < j) = (j < k)
c in hue1

6.7.2. Operators.

6.7.2.1. General.

multiplying–operator = "*" | "/" | "div" | "mod" | "and" .

adding–operator = "+" | "–" | "or" .

relational–operator = "=" | "<>" | "<" | ">" | "<=" | ">=" | "in" .

A factor, or a term, or a simple–expression shall be designated an operand. The order of evaluation of the operands of a dyadic operator shall be implementation–dependent.

NOTE: This means, for example, that the operands may be evaluated in textual order, or in reverse order, or in parallel or they may not both be evaluated.

6.7.2.2. Arithmetic Operators.

The types of operands and results for dyadic and monadic operations shall be as shown in Tables 2 and 3 respectively.

Table 2.
Dyadic Arithmetic Operations

operator	operation	type of operands	type of result
+	addition	integer–type or real–type	(1)
–	subtraction	integer–type or real–type	(1)
*	multiplication	integer–type or real–type	(1)
/	division	integer–type or real–type	real–type
div	division with truncation	integer–type	integer–type
mod	modulo	integer–type	integer–type

(1) Integer–type if both operands are of integer–type otherwise real–type.

Table 3.
Monadic Arithmetic Operations

operator	operation	type of operand	type of result
+	identity	integer–type	integer–type
		real–type	real–type
–	sign–inversion	integer–type	integer–type
		real–type	real–type

NOTE: The symbols +, – and * are also used as set operators (see 6.7.2.4).

A term of the form x/y shall be an error if y is zero, otherwise the value of x/y shall be the result of dividing x by y.

A term of the form i div j shall be an error if j is zero, otherwise the value of i div j shall be such that

$$\text{abs}(i) - \text{abs}(j) < \text{abs}((i \text{ div } j) * j) <= \text{abs}(i)$$

where the value shall be zero if abs(i) < abs(j), otherwise the sign of the value shall be positive if i and j have the same sign and negative if i and j have different signs.

A term of the form i mod j shall be an error if j is zero or negative, otherwise the value of i mod j shall be that value of (i–(k*j)) for integral k such that 0 <= i mod j < j.

NOTE: Only for i >= 0 and j > 0 does the relation (i div j) * j + i mod j = i hold.

The required constant-identifier **maxint** shall denote an implementation–defined value of integer-type. This value shall satisfy the following conditions.

(a) All integral values in the closed interval from –**maxint** to +**maxint** shall be values of the integer-type.

(b) Any monadic operation performed on an integer value in this interval shall be correctly performed according to the mathematical rules for integer arithmetic.

(c) Any dyadic integer operation on two integer values in this same interval shall be correctly performed according to the mathematical rules for integer arithmetic, provided that the result is also in this interval.

(d) Any relational operation on two integer values in this same interval shall be correctly performed according to the mathematical rules for integer arithmetic.

The results of the real arithmetic operators and functions shall be approximations to the corresponding mathematical results. The accuracy of this approximation shall be implementation–defined.

It shall be an error if an integer operation or function is not performed according to the mathematical rules for integer arithmetic.

6.7.2.3. Boolean Operators.   Operands and results for Boolean operations shall be of Boolean-type. Boolean operators **or, and** and **not** shall denote respectively the logical operations of disjunction, conjunction and negation.

Boolean-expression = expression .

A Boolean-expression shall be an expression that denotes a value of Boolean-type.

6.7.2.4. Set Operators.   The types of operands and results for set operations shall be as shown in Table 4.

6.7.2.5. Relational-Operators.   The types of operands and results for relational operations shall be as shown in Table 5.

Table 4.
Set Operations

operator	operation	type of operands	type of result
+	set union	(1)	same as the operands
−	set difference	(1)	same as the operands
*	set intersection	(1)	same as the operands

(1) a canonical set-of-T type (see 6.7.1)

The operands of $=$, $<>$, $<$, $>$, $>=$, and $<=$ shall be either of compatible types, the same canonical set-of-T type, or one operand shall be of real-type and the other shall be of integer-type.

The operators $=$, $<>$, $<$, and $>$ shall stand for *equal to, not equal to, less than* and *greater than* respectively.

Except when applied to sets, the operators $<=$ and $>=$ shall stand for *less than or equal to* and *greater than or equal to* respectively.

Table 5.
Relational Operations

operator		type of operands	type of result
=	<>	any simple, pointer or string–type or canonical set–of–T type	Boolean–type
<	>	any simple or string–type	Boolean–type
<=	>=	any simple or string–type or canonical set–of–T type	Boolean–type
in		left operand: any ordinal type T right operand: a canonical set–of–T type	Boolean–type

Where u and v denote operands of a set–type, u $<=$ v shall denote the inclusion of u in v and u $>=$ v shall denote the inclusion of v in u.

NOTE: Since the Boolean–type is an ordinal–type with false less than true, then if p and q are operands of Boolean–type, p = q denotes their equivalence and p $<=$ q means p implies q.

When the relational operators =, $<>$, $<$, $>$, $<=$, and $>=$ are used to compare operands of compatible string–types (see 6.4.3.2), they denote lexicographic relations defined below. Lexicographic ordering imposes a total ordering on values of a string–type. If s1 and s2 are two values of compatible string–types, and n denotes the number of components of the compatible string–types, then

s1 = s2 iff for all i in [1..n]: s1[i] = s2[i]

s1 $<$ s2 iff there exists a p in [1..n]: (for all i in [1..p–1]: s1[i] = s2[i])
        and s1[p] $<$ s2[p]

The operator in shall yield the value true if the value of the operand of ordinal–type is a member of the value of the set–type, otherwise it shall yield the value false.

6.7.3. Function–Designators.
A function–designator shall specify the activation of the block *of* the function–block associated with the function–identifier *of* the function–designator, and shall yield the value of the result of the activation upon completion of the algorithm of the

activation; it shall be an error if the result is undefined upon completion of the algorithm.   If the function has any formal parameters the function–designator shall *contain* a list of actual–parameters that shall be bound to their corresponding formal parameters defined in the function–declaration.   The correspondence shall be established by the positions of the parameters in the lists of actual and formal parameters respectively.   The number of actual–parameters shall be equal to the number of formal parameters. The types of the actual–parameters shall correspond to the types of the formal parameters as specified by 6.6.3. The order of evaluation, accessing and binding of the actual–parameters shall be implementation–dependent.

function–designator = function–identifier [actual–parameter–list] .

actual–parameter–list =
     "(" actual–parameter { "," actual–parameter } ")" .

actual–parameter = expression | variable–access |
                               procedure–identifier | function–identifier .

EXAMPLES:

Sum(a, 63)
GCD(147, k)
sin(x + y)
eof(f)
ord(f↑)

6.8. Statements.

6.8.1. General.   Statements shall denote algorithmic actions, and shall be executable.

NOTE: Statements may be prefixed by a label.

A label, if any, *of* a statement S shall be designated as prefixing S, and shall be allowed to occur *in* a goto–statement G (see 6.8.2.4) if and only if any of the following three conditions is satisfied.

(a) S *contains* G.

(b) S is a statement *of* a statement-sequence *containing* G.

(c) S is a statement *of* the statement-sequence *of* the compound-statement *of* the statement-part *of* a block *containing* G.

statement = [label ":"] (simple-statement | structured-statement) .

NOTE: A goto-statement within a block may refer to a label in an enclosing block, provided that the label prefixes a simple-statement or structured-statement at the outermost level of nesting of the block.

6.8.2. Simple-Statements.

6.8.2.1. General. A simple-statement shall be a statement not *containing* a statement. An empty-statement shall *contain* no symbol and shall denote no action.

simple-statement = empty-statement | assignment-statement |
procedure-statement | goto-statement .

empty-statement = .

6.8.2.2. Assignment-Statements. An assignment-statement shall attribute the value of the expression *of* the assignment-statement either to the variable denoted by the variable-access *of* the assignment-statement, or to the activation result that is denoted by the function-identifier *of* the assignment-statement; the value shall be assignment-compatible with the type possessed, respectively, by the variable or by the activation result. The function-block associated (see 6.6.2) with the function-identifier *of* an assignment-statement shall *contain* the assignment-statement.

assignment-statement =
(variable-access | function-identifier) ":=" expression .

The decision as to the order of accessing the variable and evaluating the expression shall be implementation-dependent; the access shall establish a reference to the variable during the remaining execution of the assignment-statement.

The state of a variable or activation result when the variable or activation result does not have attributed to it a value specified by its type shall be designated *undefined*. If a variable possesses a structured-type, the state of the variable when every component of the variable is totally–undefined shall be designated *totally–undefined.* Totally–undefined shall be synonymous with undefined for an activation result or a variable that does not possess a structured–type.

EXAMPLES:

```
x := y + z
p := (1 <= i) and (i < 100)
i := sqr(k) – (i * j)
hue1 := [blue, succ(c)]
p1↑.mother := true
```

6.8.2.3. Procedure–Statements.

A procedure–statement shall specify the activation of the block *of* the procedure–block associated with the procedure–identifier *of* the procedure–statement. If the procedure has any formal parameters the procedure–statement shall *contain* an actual–parameter–list, which is the list of actual–parameters that shall be bound to their corresponding formal parameters defined in the procedure–declaration. The correspondence shall be established by the positions of the parameters in the lists of actual and formal parameters respectively. The number of actual–parameters shall be equal to the number of formal parameters. The types of the actual–parameters shall correspond to the types of the formal parameters as specified by 6.6.3. The order of evaluation, accessing and binding of the actual–parameters shall be implementation–dependent.

The procedure–identifier *in* a procedure–statement *containing* a read–parameter–list shall denote the required procedure read; the procedure–identifier *in* a procedure–statement *containing* a readln–parameter–list shall denote the required procedure readln; the procedure–identifier *in* a procedure–statement *containing* a write–parameter–list shall denote the required procedure write; the procedure–identifier *in* a procedure–statement *containing* a writeln–parameter–list shall denote the required procedure writeln.

```
procedure-statement =
    procedure-identifier ( [ actual-parameter-list ] |
                            read-parameter-list |
                            readln-parameter-list |
                            write-parameter-list |
                            writeln-parameter-list ) .
```

EXAMPLES:

    printheading
    transpose(a, n, m)
    bisect(fct, –1.0, +1.0, x)

6.8.2.4. Goto–Statements.   A goto–statement shall indicate that further processing is to continue at the program–point denoted by the label *in* the goto–statement and shall cause the termination of all activations except:

(a) the activation containing the program–point; and

(b) any activation containing the activation–point of an activation required by exceptions (a) or (b) not to be terminated.

    goto-statement = "goto" label .

6.8.3. Structured–Statements.

6.8.3.1. General.

    structured-statement = compound-statement | conditional-statement |
                        repetitive-statement | with-statement .

    statement-sequence = statement { ";" statement } .

The execution of a statement–sequence shall specify the execution *of* the statements of the statement–sequence in textual order, except as modified by execution of a goto–statement.

6.8.3.2. Compound–Statements.   A compound–statement shall specify execution of the statement–sequence *of* the compound–statement.

    compound-statement = "begin" statement-sequence "end" .

EXAMPLE:

    begin z := x ; x := y ; y := z end

6.8.3.3. Conditional-Statements.

conditional-statement = if-statement | case-statement .

6.8.3.4. If-Statements.

if-statement = "if" Boolean-expression "then" statement [else-part] .

else-part = "else" statement .

If the Boolean-expression *of* the if-statement yields the value true, the statement *of* the if-statement shall be executed. If the Boolean-expression yields the value false, the statement *of* the if-statement shall not be executed and the statement *of* the else-part (if any) shall be executed.

An if-statement without an else-part shall not be immediately followed by the token else.

NOTE: An else–part is thus paired with the nearest preceding otherwise unpaired then.

EXAMPLES:

(1)   if x < 1.5 then z := x + y else z := 1.5

(2)   if p1 <> nil then p1 := p1↑.father

(3)   if j = 0 then
        if i = 0 then writeln('indefinite')
        else writeln('infinite')
      else writeln(i / j)

6.8.3.5. Case-Statements.

The values denoted by the case-constants *of* the case-constant-lists *of* the case-list-elements *of* a case-statement shall be distinct and of the same ordinal-type as the expression *of* the case-index *of* the case-statement. On execution of the case-statement the case-index shall be evaluated. That value shall then specify execution of the statement *of* the case-list-element *closest-containing* the case-constant denoting that value. One of the case-constants shall be equal to the value of the case-index upon entry to the case-statement, otherwise it shall be an error.

NOTE: Case–constants are not the same as statement labels.

```
case-statement = "case" case-index "of"
    case-list-element { ";" case-list-element } [ ";" ] "end" .
```

```
case-list-element = case-constant-list ":" statement .
```

```
case-index = expression .
```

EXAMPLE:

```
case operator of
  plus:   x := x + y;
  minus:  x := x - y;
  times:  x := x * y
end
```

6.8.3.6. Repetitive–Statements.
Repetitive–statements shall specify that certain statements are to be executed repeatedly.

```
repetitive-statement = repeat-statement |
                       while-statement |
                       for-statement .
```

6.8.3.7. Repeat–Statements.

```
repeat-statement = "repeat" statement-sequence
                   "until" Boolean-expression .
```

The statement-sequence *of* the repeat-statement shall be repeatedly executed (except as modified by the execution of a goto-statement) until the Boolean-expression *of* the repeat-statement yields the value true on completion of the statement-sequence. The statement-sequence shall be executed at least once, because the Boolean-expression is evaluated after execution of the statement-sequence.

EXAMPLE:

```
repeat k := i mod j;
  i := j;
  j := k
until j = 0
```

6.8.3.8. While–Statements.

while–statement = "while" Boolean–expression "do" statement .

The while–statement

while b do body

shall be equivalent to

```
begin
  if b then
    repeat
    body
    until not (b)
end
```

EXAMPLES:

(1)   while i > 0 do
         begin
           if odd(i) then z := z * x;
           i := i div 2;
           x := sqr(x)
         end

(2)   while not eof(f) do
         begin
           process(f↑);
           get(f)
         end

6.8.3.9. For–Statements.   The for-statement shall specify that the statement *of* the for-statement is to be repeatedly executed while a progression of values is attributed to a variable that is designated the control–variable *of* the for-statement.

for–statement = "for" control–variable ":=" initial–value
                ("to" | "downto") final–value "do" statement .

control–variable = entire–variable .

initial–value = expression .

final–value = expression .

The control–variable shall be an entire–variable whose identifier is declared in the variable–declaration–part *of* the block *closest–containing* the for–statement. The control–variable shall possess an ordinal–type, and the initial–value and final–value shall be of a type compatible with this type. The initial–value and the final–value shall be assignment–compatible with the type possessed by the control–variable if the statement *of* the for–statement is executed. After a for–statement is executed (other than being left by a goto–statement leading out of it) the control–variable shall be undefined. Neither a for–statement nor any procedure–and–function–declaration–part *of* the block that *closest–contains* a for–statement shall *contain* a statement threatening the variable denoted by the control–variable *of* the for–statement.

A statement S shall be designated as *threatening* a variable V if one or more of the following statements is true.

(a) S is an assignment–statement and V is denoted by the variable–access *of* S.

(b) S *contains* an actual variable parameter that denotes V.

(c) S is a procedure–statement that specifies the activation of the required procedure read or the required procedure readln, and V is denoted by a variable–access *of* a read–parameter–list or readln–parameter–list *of* S.

(d) S is a for–statement and the control–variable *of* S denotes V.

Apart from the restrictions imposed by these requirements, the for–statement

for v := e1 to e2 do body

shall be equivalent to

```
begin
temp1 := e1;
temp2 := e2;
if temp1 <= temp2 then
  begin
  v := temp1;
  body;
  while v <> temp2 do
    begin
    v := succ(v);
    body
    end
  end
end
```

and the for–statement

```
for v := e1 downto e2 do body
```

shall be equivalent to

```
begin
temp1 := e1;
temp2 := e2;
if temp1 >= temp2 then
  begin
  v := temp1;
  body;
  while v <> temp2 do
    begin
    v := pred(v);
    body
    end
  end
end
```

where temp1 and temp2 denote auxiliary variables that the program does
not otherwise contain, and that possess the type possessed by the variable
v if that type is not a subrange–type; otherwise the host type of the type
possessed by the variable v.

EXAMPLES:

(1) for i := 2 to 63 do
      if a[i] > max then max := a[i]

(2) for i := 1 to 10 do
      for j := 1 to 10 do
        begin
        x := 0;
        for k := 1 to 10 do
          x := x + m1[i,k] * m2[k,j];
        m[i,j] := x
        end

(3) for i := 1 to 10 do
      for j := 1 to i – 1 do
        m[i][j] := 0.0

(4) for c := blue downto red do q(c)

6.8.3.10. With–Statements.

with–statement = "with" record–variable–list "do" statement .

record–variable–list = record–variable { "," record–variable } .

field–designator–identifier = identifier .

A with–statement shall specify the execution of the statement *of* the with-statement. The occurrence of a record-variable as the only record-variable *in* the record-variable-list *of* a with-statement shall constitute a defining-point of each of the field-identifiers associated with components of the record-type possessed by the record-variable as a field-designator-identifier for the region that is the statement *of* the with-statement; each applied occurrence of a field-designator-identifier shall denote that component of the record-variable that is associated with the field-identifier by the record-type. The record-variable shall be accessed before the statement *of* the with-statement is executed, and that access shall establish a reference to the variable during the entire execution of the statement *of* the with-statement.

The statement

with $v_1, v_2, ..., v_n$ do s

shall be equivalent to

with v_1 do
  with v_2 do
    ...
      with v_n do s

EXAMPLE:

```
with date do
  if month = 12 then
    begin month := 1; year := year + 1
    end
  else month := month+1
```

has the same effect on the variable date as

```
if date.month = 12 then
  begin date.month := 1; date.year := date.year+1
  end
else date.month := date.month+1
```

6.9. Input and Output.

6.9.1. The Procedure Read.
The syntax of the parameter list of read when applied to a textfile shall be:

```
read-parameter-list =
    "(" [ file-variable "," ] variable-access { "," variable-access } ")" .
```

If the file-variable is omitted, the procedure shall be applied to the required textfile input.

The following requirements shall apply for the procedure read (where f denotes a textfile and $v_1...v_n$ denote variable-accesses possessing the char-type (or a subrange of char-type), the integer-type (or a subrange of integer-type), or the real-type).

(a) read(f,v_1,...,v_n) shall access the textfile variable and establish a reference to that textfile variable for the remaining execution of the statement. The execution of the statement shall be equivalent to

> begin read(ff,v_1);   read(ff,v_2,...,v_n) end

where ff denotes the referenced textfile variable. The read statement containing v_1 shall be executed before accessing the variables v_2,...,v_n.

(b) If v is a variable–access possessing the char–type (or subrange thereof), read(f,v) shall access the textfile variable and establish a reference to that textfile variable for the remaining execution of the statement. The execution of the statement shall be equivalent to

> begin v := ff↑;   get(ff) end

where ff denotes the referenced textfile variable.

NOTE: The variable–access is not a variable parameter. Consequently it may be a component of a packed structure and the value of the buffer–variable need only be assignment–compatible with it.

(c) If v is a variable–access possessing the integer–type (or subrange thereof), read(f,v) shall access the textfile variable and establish a reference to that textfile variable for the remaining execution of the statement. The remaining execution of the statement shall cause the reading from the referenced textfile variable of a sequence of characters. Preceding spaces and end–of–lines shall be skipped. It shall be an error if the rest of the sequence does not form a signed–integer according to the syntax of 6.1.5. Reading shall cease as soon as the buffer–variable of the referenced textfile does not have attributed to it a character contained by the signed–integer. The value of the signed–integer thus read shall be assignment–compatible with the type possessed by v, and shall be attributed to v.

(d) If v is a variable–access possessing the real–type, read(f,v) shall access the textfile variable and establish a reference to that textfile variable for the remaining execution of the statement. The remaining execution of the statement shall cause the reading from the referenced textfile variable of a sequence of characters. Preceding spaces and end–of–lines shall be skipped. It shall be an error if the rest of the sequence does not form a signed–number according to the syntax of 6.1.5. Reading shall cease as soon as the buffer–variable of the referenced textfile does not have attributed to it a character contained by the signed–number. The value denoted by the number thus read shall be attributed to the variable v.

(e) When read is applied to f, it shall be an error if the buffer–variable f↑ is undefined or the pre–assertions for get do not hold (see 6.4.3.5).

6.9.2. The Procedure Readln.

The syntax of the parameter list of readln shall be:

readln–parameter–list =
    ["(" (file–variable | variable–access) { "," variable–access } ")"] .

Readln shall only be applied to textfiles. If the file–variable or the entire readln–parameter–list is omitted, the procedure shall be applied to the required textfile input.

Readln(f,v_1,...,v_n) shall access the textfile variable and establish a reference to that textfile variable for the remaining execution of the statement. The execution of the statement shall be equivalent to

begin read(ff,v_1,...,v_n); readln(ff) end

where ff denotes the referenced textfile variable.

readln(f) shall access the textfile variable and establish a reference to that textfile variable for the remaining execution of the statement. The execution of the statement shall be equivalent to

begin while not eoln(ff) do get(ff); get(ff) end

where ff denotes the referenced text file variable.

NOTE: The effect of readln is to place the current file position just past the end of the current line in the textfile. Unless this is the end–of–file position, the current file position is therefore at the start of the next line.

6.9.3. The Procedure Write.

The syntax of the parameter list of write when applied to a textfile shall be:

write–parameter–list =
    "(" [file–variable ","] write–parameter { "," write–parameter } ")" .

write–parameter = expression [":" expression [":" expression]] .

If the file-variable is omitted, the procedure shall be applied to the required textfile output. When write is applied to a textfile f, it shall be an error if f is undefined or f.M = Inspection (see 6.4.3.5). An application of write to a textfile f shall cause the buffer-variable f↑ to become undefined.

Write(f,p_1,....,p_n) shall access the textfile variable and establish a reference to that textfile variable for the remaining execution of the statement. The execution of the statement shall be equivalent to

begin write(ff,p_1); write(ff,p_2,....,p_n) end

where ff denotes the referenced textfile variable. The write statement containing p_1 shall be executed before evaluating the write-parameters p_2,....,p_n.

6.9.3.1. Write-Parameters.

The write-parameters p shall have the following forms:

e : TotalWidth : FracDigits   e : TotalWidth   e

where e is an expression whose value is to be written on the file f and may be of integer-type, real-type, char-type, Boolean-type or a string-type, and where *TotalWidth* and *FracDigits* are expressions of integer-type whose values are the field-width parameters. The values of *TotalWidth* and *FracDigits* shall be greater than or equal to one; it shall be an error if either value is less than one.

Write(f,e) shall be equivalent to the form write(f,e : TotalWidth), using a default value for *TotalWidth* that depends on the type of e; for integer-type, real-type and Boolean-type the default values shall be implementation-defined.

Write(f,e : TotalWidth : FracDigits) shall be applicable only if e is of real-type (see 6.9.3.4.2).

6.9.3.2. Char-Type.

If e is of char-type, the default value of *TotalWidth* shall be one. The representation written on the file f shall be:

(TotalWidth − 1) spaces, the character value of e.

6.9.3.3. Integer–Type. If e is of integer–type, the decimal representation of e shall be written on the file f. Assume a function

```
function IntegerSize ( x : integer ) : integer ;
  { returns the number of digits, z, such that
     10 to the power (z–1) <= abs(x) < 10 to the power z }
```

and let *IntDigits* be the positive integer defined by:

```
if e = 0
then IntDigits := 1
else IntDigits := IntegerSize(e);
```

then the representation shall consist of:

(a) if TotalWidth >= IntDigits + 1:
     (TotalWidth – IntDigits – 1) spaces,
     the sign character: '–' if e < 0, otherwise a space,
     IntDigits digit–characters of the decimal representation of abs(e).

(b) If TotalWidth < IntDigits + 1:
     if e < 0 the sign character '–',
     IntDigits digit–characters of the decimal representation of abs(e).

6.9.3.4. Real–Type. If e is of real–type, a decimal representation of the number e, rounded to the specified number of significant figures or decimal places, shall be written on the file f.

6.9.3.4.1. The Floating–Point Representation.
Write(f,e : TotalWidth) shall cause a floating–point representation of e to be written. Assume functions

```
function TenPower ( Int : integer ) : real ;
  { Returns 10.0 raised to the power Int }

function RealSize ( y : real ) : integer ;
  { Returns the value, z, such that
    TenPower(z–1) <= abs(y) < TenPower(z) }

function Truncate ( y : real ; DecPlaces : integer ) : real ;
  { Returns the value of y after truncation
    to DecPlaces decimal places }
```

let *ExpDigits* be an implementation–defined value representing the number of digit–characters written in an exponent;

let *ActWidth* be the positive integer defined by:

  if TotalWidth >= ExpDigits + 6
    then ActWidth := TotalWidth
    else ActWidth := ExpDigits + 6;

and let the non–negative number *eWritten*, the positive integer *DecPlaces* and the integer *ExpValue* be defined by:

  DecPlaces := ActWidth – ExpDigits – 5;
  if e = 0.0
    then begin eWritten := 0.0; ExpValue := 0 end
    else
    begin
    eWritten := abs(e);
    ExpValue := RealSize (eWritten) – 1;
    eWritten := eWritten / TenPower (ExpValue);
    eWritten := eWritten + 0.5 * TenPower (–DecPlaces);
    if eWritten >= 10.0
      then
      begin
      eWritten := eWritten / 10.0;
      ExpValue := ExpValue + 1
      end;
    eWritten := Truncate (eWritten, DecPlaces)
    end;

then the floating–point representation of the value of e shall consist of:

    the sign character
      ('–' if (e < 0) and (eWritten > 0), otherwise a space),
    the leading digit–character of the decimal representation of eWritten,
    the character '.' ,
    the next DecPlaces digit–characters of the decimal representation of
      eWritten,
    an implementation–defined exponent character
      (either 'e' or 'E'),

the sign of ExpValue
('–' if ExpValue < 0, otherwise '+'),
the ExpDigits digit–characters of the decimal representation of
ExpValue (with leading zeros if the value requires them).

6.9.3.4.2. The Fixed–Point Representation.

Write(f,e : TotalWidth : FracDigits) shall cause a fixed–point representation of e to be written. Assume the functions TenPower and Truncate described in 6.9.3.4.1;

let eWritten be the non–negative number defined by:

```
if e = 0.0
  then eWritten := 0.0
  else
  begin
    eWritten := abs(e);
    eWritten := eWritten + 0.5 * TenPower ( - FracDigits );
    eWritten := Truncate ( eWritten, FracDigits )
  end;
```

let IntDigits be the positive integer defined by:

```
if RealSize ( eWritten ) < 1
  then IntDigits := 1
  else IntDigits := RealSize ( eWritten );
```

and let MinNumChars be the positive integer defined by:

```
MinNumChars := IntDigits + FracDigits + 1;
  if (e < 0.0) and (eWritten > 0)
    then MinNumChars := MinNumChars + 1; {'-' required}
```

then the fixed-point representation of the value of e shall consist of:

if TotalWidth >= MinNumChars,
   (TotalWidth - MinNumChars) spaces,
the character '-' if (e < 0) and (eWritten > 0),
the first IntDigits digit-characters of the decimal representation of
   the value of eWritten,
the character '.',
the next FracDigits digit-characters of the decimal representation of
   the value of eWritten.

NOTE: At least *MinNumChars* characters are written. If *TotalWidth* is less than this value, no initial spaces are written.

6.9.3.5. Boolean-Type.

If e is of Boolean-type, a representation of the word true or the word false (as appropriate to the value of e) shall be written on the file f. This shall be equivalent to writing the appropriate character-strings 'True' or 'False' (see 6.9.3.6), where the case of each letter is implementation-defined, with a field-width parameter of *TotalWidth*.

6.9.3.6. String-Types.

If the type of e is a string-type with n components, the default value of *TotalWidth* shall be n. The representation shall consist of:

if TotalWidth > n,
   (TotalWidth - n) spaces,
   the first through n-th characters of the value of e in that order.

if 1 <= TotalWidth <= n,
   the first through TotalWidth-th characters in that order.

6.9.4. The Procedure Writeln.

The syntax of the parameter list of writeln shall be:

writeln-parameter-list = ["(" (file-variable | write-parameter)
                              | "," write-parameter | ")"] .

Writeln shall only be applied to textfiles. If the file-variable or the writeln-parameter-list is omitted, the procedure shall be applied to the required textfile output.

Writeln($f,p_1,...,p_n$) shall access the textfile variable and establish a reference to that textfile variable for the remaining execution of the statement. The execution of the statement shall be equivalent to

$$\text{begin write(ff,} p_1,...,p_n\text{); writeln(ff) end}$$

where ff denotes the referenced textfile variable.

Writeln shall be defined by a pre–assertion and a post–assertion using the notation of 6.6.5.2.

pre–assertion: (f0 is not undefined) and (f0.M = Generation) and (f0.R = S()).

post–assertion: (f.L = (f0.L $\sim$ S(e))) and
(f↑ is totally–undefined) and
(f.R = S()) and (f.M = Generation),
where S(e) is the sequence consisting solely of the end–of–line component defined in 6.4.3.5.

NOTE: Writeln(f) terminates the partial line, if any, which is being generated. By the conventions of 6.6.5.2 it is an error if the pre–assertion is not true prior to writeln(f).

6.9.5. The Procedure Page.

It shall be an error if the pre–assertion required for writeln(f) (see 6.9.4) does not hold prior to the activation of page(f). If the actual–parameter–list is omitted the procedure shall be applied to the required textfile output. Page(f) shall cause an implementation–defined effect on the textfile f, such that subsequent text written to f will be on a new page if the textfile is printed on a suitable device, shall perform an implicit writeln(f) if f.L is not empty and if f.L.last is not the end–of–line component (see 6.4.3.5), and shall cause the buffer–variable f↑ to become totally–undefined. The effect of inspecting a textfile to which the page procedure was applied during generation shall be implementation–dependent.

6.10. Programs.

program = program–heading ";" program–block "." .

program–heading =
"program" identifier ["(" program–parameters ")"] .

program–parameters = identifier–list .

program–block = block .

The identifier *of* the program–heading shall be the program name that shall have no significance within the program. The identifiers *contained* by the program–parameters shall be distinct and shall be designated program parameters. Each program parameter shall have a defining–point as a variable–identifier for the region that is the program–block. The binding of the variables denoted by the program parameters to entities external to the program shall be implementation–dependent, except if the variable possesses a file–type in which case the binding shall be implementation–defined.

NOTE: The external representation of such external entities is not defined by this standard, nor is any property of a Pascal program dependent on such representation.

The occurrence of the required identifier input or the required identifier output as a program parameter shall constitute its defining–point for the region that is the program–block as a variable–identifier of the required type denoted by the required type–identifier text. Such occurrence of the identifier input shall cause the post–assertions of reset to hold, and of output, the post–assertions of rewrite to hold, prior to the first access to the textfile or its associated buffer–variable. The effect of the application of the required procedure reset or the required procedure rewrite to either of these textfiles shall be implementation–defined.

EXAMPLES:

(1)
```
program copy (f, g);
var f, g : file of real;
begin reset(f); rewrite(g);
   while not eof(f) do
      begin g↑ := f↑; get(f); put(g)
      end
end.
```

(2)
```
program copytext (input, output);
   {This program copies the characters and line structure of the
   textfile input to the textfile output.}
var ch : char;
begin
   while not eof do
   begin
      while not eoln do
         begin read(ch); write(ch)
         end;
      readln; writeln
   end
end.
```

```
(3)   program t6p6p3p4 (output);
      var globalone, globaltwo : integer;

      procedure dummy;
        begin
        writeln('fail4')
        end { of dummy };

      procedure p (procedure f(procedure ff; procedure gg); procedure g);
        var localtop : integer;
        procedure r;
          begin
          if globalone = 1 then
            begin
            if (globaltwo <> 2) or (localtop <> 1) then
                writeln('fail1')
            end
          else if globalone = 2 then
            begin
            if (globaltwo <> 2) or (localtop <> 2) then
                writeln('fail2')
            else writeln('pass')
            end
          else writeln('fail3');
          globalone := globalone + 1
          end { of r };
        begin { of p }
        globaltwo := globaltwo + 1;
        localtop := globaltwo;
        if globaltwo = 1 then
          p(f, r)
        else
          f(g, r)
        end { of p};

      procedure q (procedure f; procedure g);
        begin
        f;
        g
        end { of q};
```

```
begin
globalone := 1;
globaltwo := 0;
p(q, dummy)
end.
```

Appendices

(These Appendices are not a part of ANSI/IEEE770X3.97–1983, IEEE Standard Pascal Computer Programming Language.)

Appendix A

Collected Syntax

The non-terminal symbols pointer-type, program, signed-number, simple-type, special-symbol and structured-type are only referenced by the semantics and are not used in the right-hand-side of any production. The non-terminal symbol *program* is the start symbol of the grammar.

actual-parameter = expression | variable-access |
       procedure-identifier | function-identifier .

actual-parameter-list =
  "(" actual-parameter { "," actual-parameter } ")" .

adding-operator = "+" | "-" | "or" .

apostrophe-image = "''" .

array-type =
  "array" "[" index-type { "," index-type } "]" "of" component-type .

array-variable = variable-access .

assignment-statement =
 (variable-access | function-identifier) ":=" expression .

base-type = ordinal-type .

block = label–declaration–part
           constant–definition–part
            type–definition–part
             variable–declaration–part
              procedure–and–function–declaration–part
              statement–part .

Boolean–expression = expression .

buffer–variable = file–variable "↑" .

case–constant = constant .

case–constant–list = case–constant { "," case–constant } .

case–index = expression .

case–list–element = case–constant–list ":" statement .

case–statement =
    "case" case–index "of"
    case–list–element { ";" case–list–element } [";"] "end" .

character–string = "" string–element { string–element } "" .

component–type = type–denoter .

component–variable = indexed–variable | field–designator .

compound–statement = "begin" statement–sequence "end" .

conditional–statement = if–statement | case–statement .

constant = [sign] (unsigned–number | constant–identifier) |
        character–string .

constant–definition = identifier "=" constant .

constant–definition–part =
    ["const" constant–definition ";" { constant–definition ";" }] .

.

constant–identifier = identifier .

control–variable = entire–variable .

digit = "0" | "1" | "2" | "3" | "4" | "5" | "6" | "7" | "8" | "9" .

digit–sequence = digit { digit } .

directive = letter { letter | digit } .

domain–type = type–identifier .

else–part = "else" statement .

empty–statement = .

entire–variable = variable–identifier .

enumerated–type = "(" identifier–list ")" .

expression =
      simple–expression [relational–operator simple–expression] .

factor = variable–access | unsigned–constant |
      function–designator | set–constructor |
      "(" expression ")" | "not" factor .

field–designator = record–variable "." field–specifier |
             field–designator–identifier .

field–designator–identifier = identifier .

field–identifier = identifier .

field–list = [(fixed–part [";" variant–part] | variant–part) [";"]] .

field–specifier = field–identifier .

file–type = "file" "of" component–type .

file–variable = variable–access .

final–value = expression .

fixed–part = record–section { ";" record–section } .

for–statement = "for" control–variable ":=" initial–value
("to" | "downto") final–value "do" statement .

formal–parameter–list =
"(" formal–parameter–section { ";" formal–parameter–section } ")" .

formal–parameter–section = value–parameter–specification |
variable–parameter–specification |
procedural–parameter–specification |
functional–parameter–specification .

fractional–part = digit–sequence .

function–block = block .

function–declaration = function–heading ";" directive |
function–identification ";" function–block |
function–heading ";" function–block .

function–designator = function–identifier [actual–parameter–list] .

function–heading =
"function" identifier [formal–parameter–list] ":" result–type .

function–identification = "function" function–identifier .

function–identifier = identifier .

functional–parameter–specification = function–heading .

goto–statement = "goto" label .

identified–variable = pointer–variable "↑" .

identifier = letter { letter | digit } .

identifier–list = identifier { "," identifier } .

if–statement = "if" Boolean–expression "then" statement [else–part] .

index–expression = expression .

index–type = ordinal–type .

indexed–variable =
     array–variable "[" index–expression { "," index–expression } "]" .

initial–value = expression .

label = digit–sequence .

label–declaration–part = ["label" label { "," label } ";"] .

letter = "a" | "b" | "c" | "d" | "e" | "f" | "g" | "h" | "i" | "j" | "k" | "l" | "m" |
     "n" | "o" | "p" | "q" | "r" | "s" | "t" | "u" | "v" | "w" | "x" | "y" | "z" .

member–designator = expression [".." expression] .

multiplying–operator = "*" | "/" | "div" | "mod" | "and" .

new–ordinal–type = enumerated–type | subrange–type .

new–pointer–type = "↑" domain–type .

new–structured–type = ["packed"] unpacked–structured–type .

new–type = new–ordinal–type | new–structured–type | new–pointer–type .

ordinal–type = new–ordinal–type | ordinal–type–identifier .

ordinal–type–identifier = type–identifier .

pointer–type = new–pointer–type | pointer–type–identifier .

pointer-type-identifier = type-identifier .

pointer-variable = variable-access .

procedural-parameter-specification = procedure-heading .

procedure-and-function-declaration-part =
     { (procedure-declaration | function-declaration) ";" } .

procedure-block = block .

procedure-declaration = procedure-heading ";" directive |
                  procedure-identification ";" procedure-block |
                  procedure-heading ";" procedure-block .

procedure-heading = "procedure" identifier [formal-parameter-list] .

procedure-identification = "procedure" procedure-identifier .

procedure-identifier = identifier .

procedure-statement = procedure-identifier ([actual-parameter-list] |
                          read-parameter-list |
                          readln-parameter-list |
                          write-parameter-list |
                          writeln-parameter-list) .

program = program-heading ";" program-block "." .

program-block = block .

program-heading = "program" identifier ["(" program-parameters ")"] .

program-parameters = identifier-list .

read-parameter-list =
     "(" [file-variable ","] variable-access { "," variable-access } ")" .

readln-parameter-list =
     ["(" (file-variable | variable-access) { "," variable-access } ")"] .

real–type–identifier = type–identifier .

record–section = identifier–list ":" type–denoter .

record–type = "record" field–list "end" .

record–variable = variable–access .

record–variable–list = record–variable { "," record–variable } .

relational–operator = "=" | "<>" | "<" | ">" | "<=" | ">=" | "in" .

repeat–statement = "repeat" statement–sequence
                                "until" Boolean–expression .

repetitive–statement = repeat–statement |
                                while–statement |
                                for–statement .

result–type = simple–type–identifier | pointer–type–identifier .

scale–factor = signed–integer .

set–constructor =
     "[" [member–designator { "," member–designator }] "]" .

set–type = "set" "of" base–type .

sign = "+" | "–" .

signed–integer = [sign] unsigned–integer .

signed–number = signed–integer | signed–real .

signed–real = [sign] unsigned–real .

simple–expression = [sign] term { adding–operator term } .

simple–statement = empty–statement | assignment–statement |
                                procedure–statement | goto–statement .

simple–type = ordinal–type | real–type–identifier .

simple–type–identifier = type–identifier .\

special–symbol = "+" | "–" | "*" | "/" | "=" | "<" | ">" | "[" |
"]" | "." | "," | ":" | ";" | "↑" | "(" | ")" | "<>" |
"<=" | ">=" | ":=" | ".." | word–symbol .

statement = [label ":"] (simple–statement | structured–statement) .

statement–part = compound–statement .

statement–sequence = statement { ";" statement } .

string–character = one–of–a–set–of–implementation–defined–characters .

string–element = apostrophe–image | string–character .

structured–statement = compound–statement | conditional–statement |
repetitive–statement | with–statement .

structured–type = new–structured–type | structured–type–identifier .

structured–type–identifier = type–identifier .

subrange–type = constant ".." constant .

tag–field = identifier .

tag–type = ordinal–type–identifier .

term = factor { multiplying–operator factor } .

type–definition = identifier "=" type–denoter .

type–definition–part =
["type" type–definition ";" { type–definition ";" }] .

type–denoter = type–identifier | new–type .

type–identifier = identifier .

unpacked–structured–type = array–type | record–type |
set–type | file–type .

unsigned–constant = unsigned–number | character–string |
constant–identifier | "nil .

unsigned–integer = digit–sequence .

unsigned–number = unsigned–integer | unsigned–real .

unsigned–real = unsigned–integer "." fractional–part ["e" scale–factor] |
unsigned–integer "e" scale–factor .

value–parameter–specification = identifier–list ":" type–identifier .

variable–access = entire–variable | component–variable |
identified–variable | buffer–variable .

variable–declaration = identifier–list ":" type–denoter .

variable–declaration–part =
["var" variable–declaration ";" { variable–declaration ";" }] .

variable–identifier = identifier .

variable–parameter–specification =
"var" identifier–list ":" type–identifier .

variant = case–constant–list ":" "(" field–list ")" .

variant–part = "case" variant–selector "of"
variant { ";" variant } .

variant–selector = [tag–field ":"] tag–type .

while–statement = "while" Boolean–expression "do" statement .

with-statement = "with" record-variable-list "do" statement .

word-symbol = "and" | "array" | "begin" | "case" | "const" | "div" |
                "do" | "downto" | "else" | "end" | "file" | "for" |
                "function" | "goto" | "if" | "in" | "label" | "mod" |
                "nil" | "not" | "of" | "or" | "packed" | "procedure" |
                "program" | "record" | "repeat" | "set" | "then" |
                "to" | "type" | "until" | "var" | "while" | "with" .

write-parameter = expression [":" expression [":" expression]] .

write-parameter-list = "(" [file-variable ","] write-parameter
                { "," write-parameter } ")" .

writeln-parameter-list = ["(" (file-variable | write-parameter)
                { "," write-parameter } ")"] .

Appendix B

Index

Appendix C

Required Identifiers

Identifier	Reference(s)	Identifier	Reference(s)
abs	6.6.6.2	pack	6.6.5.4
arctan	6.6.6.2	page	6.9.5
Boolean	6.4.2.2	pred	6.6.6.4
char	6.4.2.2	put	6.6.5.2
chr	6.6.6.4	read	6.6.5.2, 6.9.1
cos	6.6.6.2	readln	6.9.2
dispose	6.6.5.3	real	6.4.2.2
eof	6.6.6.5	reset	6.6.5.2
eoln	6.6.6.5	rewrite	6.6.5.2
exp	6.6.6.2	round	6.6.6.3
false	6.4.2.2	sin	6.6.6.2
get	6.6.5.2	sqr	6.6.6.2
input	6.10	sqrt	6.6.6.2
integer	6.4.2.2	succ	6.6.6.4
ln	6.6.6.2	text	6.4.3.5
maxint	6.7.2.2	true	6.4.2.2
new	6.6.5.3	trunc	6.6.6.3
odd	6.6.6.5	unpack	6.6.5.4
ord	6.6.6.4	write	6.6.5.2, 6.9.3
output	6.10	writeln	6.9.4

Appendix D

Errors

A complying processor is required to provide documentation concerning its treatment of errors. To facilitate the production of such documentation, all the errors specified in Section 6 are described again in this appendix.

1. For an indexed-variable *closest-containing* a single index-expression, it is an error if the value of the index-expression is not assignment-compatible with the index-type of the array-type.

2. It is an error unless a variant is active for the entirety of each reference and access to each component of the variant.

3. It is an error if the pointer-variable *of* an identified-variable denotes a nil-value.

4. It is an error if the pointer-variable *of* an identified-variable is undefined.

5. It is an error to remove from its pointer-type the identifying-value *of* an identified-variable when a reference to the identified variable exists.

6. It is an error to alter the value of a file-variable f when a reference to the buffer-variable f↑ exists.

7. For a value parameter, it is an error if the actual-parameter is an expression of an ordinal-type whose value is not assignment-compatible with the type possessed by the formal parameter.

8. For a value parameter, it is an error if the actual-parameter is an expression of a set-type whose value is not assignment-compatible with the type possessed by the formal parameter.

9. It is an error if the file mode is not Generation immediately prior to any use of put, write, writeln or page.

10. It is an error if the file is undefined immediately prior to any use of put, write, writeln or page.

11. It is an error if end of file is not true immediately prior to any use of put, write (or writeln or page).

12. It is an error if the buffer-variable is undefined immediately prior to any use of put.

13. It is an error if the file is undefined immediately prior to any use of reset.

14. It is an error if the file mode is not Inspection immediately prior to any use of get or read.

15. It is an error if the file is undefined immediately prior to any use of get or read.

16. It is an error if end of file is true immediately prior to any use of get or read.

17. For read, it is an error if the value possessed by the buffer-variable is not assignment-compatible with the variable-access.

18. For write, it is an error if the value possessed by the expression is not assignment-compatible with the buffer-variable.

19. For $new(p,c_1,...,c_n)$, it is an error if a variant *of* a variant-part within the new variable becomes active and a different variant of the variant-part is one of the specified variants.

20. For dispose(p), it is an error if the identifying-value had been created using the form $new(p,c_1,...,c_n)$.

21. For $dispose(p,k_1,...,k_m)$, it is an error if the variable had been created using the form $new(p,c_1,...,c_n)$ and m is not equal to n.

22. For $dispose(p,k_1,...,k_m)$, it is an error if the variants in the variable identified by the pointer value of p are different from those specified by the case-constants $k_1,...,k_m$.

23. For dispose, it is an error if the parameter of a pointer-type has a nil-value.

24. For dispose, it is an error if the parameter of a pointer-type is undefined.

25. It is an error if a variable created using the second form *of* new is accessed by the identified-variable *of* the variable-access *of* a factor, *of* an assignment-statement, or *of* an actual-parameter.

26. For pack, it is an error if the parameter of ordinal-type is not assignment-compatible with the index-type of the unpacked array parameter.

27. For pack, it is an error if any of the components of the unpacked array are both undefined and accessed.

28. For pack, it is an error if the index-type of the unpacked array is exceeded.

29. For unpack, it is an error if the parameter of ordinal-type is not assignment-compatible with the index-type of the unpacked array parameter.

30. For unpack, it is an error if any of the components of the packed array are undefined.

31. For unpack, it is an error if the index-type of the unpacked array is exceeded.

32. Sqr(x) computes the square of x. It is an error if such a value does not exist.

33. For ln(x), it is an error if x is not greater than zero.

34. For sqrt(x), it is an error if x is negative.

35. For trunc(x), the value of trunc(x) is such that if x is positive or zero then $0 <= x-\text{trunc}(x) < 1$; otherwise $-1 < x-\text{trunc}(x) <= 0$. It is an error if such a value does not exist.

36. For round(x), if x is positive or zero then round(x) is equivalent to trunc(x+0.5), otherwise round(x) is equivalent to trunc(x–0.5). It is an error if such a value does not exist.

37. For chr(x), the function returns a result of char–type which is the value whose ordinal number is equal to the value of the expression x if such a character value exists. It is an error if such a character value does not exist.

38. For succ(x), the function yields a value whose ordinal number is one greater than that of x, if such a value exists. It is an error if such a value does not exist.

39. For pred(x), the function yields a value whose ordinal number is one less than that of x, if such a value exists. It is an error if such a value does not exist.

40. When eof(f) is activated, it is an error if f is undefined.

41. When eoln(f) is activated, it is an error if f is undefined.

42. When eoln(f) is activated, it is an error if eof(f) is true.

43. An expression denotes a value unless a variable denoted by a variable–access *contained* by the expression is undefined at the time of its use, in which case that use is an error.

44. A term of the form x/y is an error if y is zero.

45. A term of the form i div j is an error if j is zero.

46. A term of the form i mod j is an error if j is zero or negative.

47. It is an error if an integer operation or function is not performed according to the mathematical rules for integer arithmetic.

48. It is an error if the result of an activation of a function is undefined upon completion of the algorithm of the activation.

49. For an assignment-statement, it is an error if the expression is of an ordinal–type whose value is not assignment–compatible with the type possessed by the variable or function–identifier.

50. For an assignment-statement, it is an error if the expression is of a set–type whose value is not assignment–compatible with the type possessed by the variable.

51. For a case-statement, it is an error if none of the case–constants is equal to the value of the case–index upon entry to the case–statement.

52. For a for-statement, it is an error if the value of the initial–value is not assignment–compatible with the type possessed by the control–variable if the statement of the for–statement is executed.

53. For a for-statement, it is an error if the value of the final–value is not assignment–compatible with the type possessed by the control–variable if the statement of the for–statement is executed.

54. On reading an integer from a textfile, after skipping preceding spaces and end–of–lines, it is an error if the rest of the sequence does not form a signed–integer.

55. On reading an integer from a textfile, it is an error if the value of the signed–integer read is not assignment–compatible with the type possessed by variable-access.

56. On reading a number from a textfile, after skipping preceding spaces and end–of–lines, it is an error if the rest of the sequence does not form a signed–number.

57. It is an error if the buffer-variable is undefined immediately prior to any use of read.

58. On writing to a textfile, the values of *TotalWidth* and *FracDigits* are greater than or equal to one; it is an error if either value is less than one.